Among The Elk

D1456689

Among
Wilderness Images
The Elk

Text by David Petersen   Photographs by Alan D. Carey

Cover photo: Two bulls at sunrise.
National Bison Refuge, Montana

Title page: Bull in early morning fog,
Yellowstone National Park, Wyoming

Text copyright © 1988 by David Petersen
Photographs copyright © 1988 by Alan Carey
All Rights Reserved.
This book may not be reproduced in whole or in part, by any means
(with the exception of short quotes for the purpose of review),
without permission of the publisher. For information, address
Northland Publishing Co., P. O. Box 1389, Flagstaff, Arizona 86002.
First Edition
Third Printing, 1993
ISBN 0-87358-476-7
Library of Congress Catalog Card Number 88-60918
4-93/5M/0449

Petersen, David.
    Among the elk: wilderness images / text by
David Petersen; photographs by Alan Carey.
        129p. cm.
        Bibliography: p. 115
        ISBN 0-87358-476-7
        1. Elk.   I. Carey, Alan.   II. Title
    QL737.U55P47 1988   88-60918
    599.73'57—dc19   CIP

Printed in Hong Kong by Colorcorp, Inc.

Dedication

This book is dedicated to the Rocky Mountain Elk Foundation.

Although I say little about the RMEF per se in the text following, I frequently cite the work of their staff and members. It seems appropriate, then, to offer here a brief introduction.

The Rocky Mountain Elk Foundation, headquartered at Missoula, Montana, is to America's elk what Ducks Unlimited is to our migratory waterfowl and Trout Unlimited to our rainbows, brookies, German browns, and native cutthroats. Founded in May 1984, the nonprofit group presently boasts a membership of more than 68,000. In the foundation's own words:

"The Rocky Mountain Elk Foundation is an international, nonprofit conservation organization dedicated to the promotion of the elk resource and the preservation and improvement of elk habitat in North America. The foundation's objectives are to:

1. Perpetuate wild, free-ranging elk populations, well balanced in age and sex, which may be hunted and otherwise enjoyed by people.

2. Encourage sound management of elk and elk habitat based on objective, scientifically based data.

3. Foster cooperation among federal, state, provincial and private organizations in managing elk.

4. Inform and involve concerned sportsmen about specific issues affecting elk hunting, management and habitat preservation.

"The RMEF's primary course of action is to raise funds from private sources to support 'on-the-ground' projects which benefit elk and elk habitat. Examples include management-related research, elk transplants to areas of suitable habitat, habitat acquisitions and habitat improvement projects."

To date, RMEF has raised more than $30 million for elk, and conserved and/or enhanced in excess of 1.1 million acres of critical wildlife habitat.

In addition to actively and successfully pursuing the objectives outlined above, RMEF publishes the attractive, informative, and highly respected magazine *Bugle: The Quarterly Journal of the Rocky Mountain Elk Foundation.*

If the foundation's references to elk hunting turn you off, please read on, for it's the shared belief of wildlife photographer Alan Carey and myself that all those who admire wild elk and wish to guarantee their future in North America—hunters, nonhunters, and antihunters alike— must join forces, if not hands, in the fight against habitat loss.

This is not a book about elk hunting, nor is it a book against elk hunting; it is a book about elk appreciation. Still, to fail to discuss the significant role hunting plays in the management and general welfare of wild elk today would be an unforgivable error of omission in any elk book that strives to be complete. There is much wrong with hunting in America today. But, no matter your personal views on the morality of the blood sports, there is also much right with hunting, especially as it affects the numbers and overall welfare of our wildlife.

There are a great many nonhunters on the rolls of the Rocky Mountain Elk Foundation, though its membership is composed primarily of conservation-minded sportsmen who, while wanting very much to maintain and improve their opportunities to enjoy quality elk hunting and the adventure and wilderness experience this challenging backcountry sport entails, want even more to assure the perpetuation of wild elk for the enjoyment of future generations of Americans.

Contents

ACKNOWLEDGMENTS ix

INTRODUCTION 1

CHAPTER ONE   Elk In North America: *Continental Images* 5

CHAPTER TWO   Elk And The Indians: *Historical Images* 13

CHAPTER THREE   Among The Elk In Rut: *Personal Images* 23

CHAPTER FOUR   Antlers: *Anatomical Images* 39

CHAPTER FIVE   Elk At Vermejo: *Research Images* 47

CHAPTER SIX   Among The Elk In Winter: *Chilling Images* 55

CHAPTER SEVEN   Among The Elk In The P-J: *Management Images* ... 65

CHAPTER EIGHT   Among The Cows And Their Calves: *Maternal Images* ... 79

CHAPTER NINE   Death Among The Elk: *Passing Images* 89

CHAPTER TEN   You Among The Elk: *Close-Up Images* 99

POSTSCRIPT 109

APPENDIX   *Recommended Reading And Viewing* 113

BIBLIOGRAPHY 115

Acknowledgments

The author wishes to express his gratitude to the following individuals for their assistance in researching and verifying the information contained in the text: wildlife biologists Alan Christensen and Gary Wolfe for providing invaluable technical information, as well as for reading the manuscript in progress and offering incisive suggestions for its improvement; District Wildlife Manager Cary Carron of the Colorado Division of Wildlife, Durango, Colorado, and U.S. Forest Service Land Manager Ron Klatt of the Pine Ranger District, Bayfield, Colorado, for taking me afield with them and answering candidly my endless questions; Bruce Woods, for his trust and support; and especially I wish to thank Carolyn, my best friend, my most candid critic, my wife.

Cow and calf. Yellowstone National Park, Woming

Introduction

Peat bogs have proven to be among nature's most efficient vaults for the long-term storage of organic matter. The peat-marsh environment's near-neutral pH, high concentrations of bone-decalcifying minerals, and subaquatic exclusion of oxygen combine to form a pickling, mummifying, and fossilizing medium far superior to any embalming brew or storage technique ever invented — the highly skilled tomb-builders and morticians of ancient Egypt notwithstanding.

From bogs in northern Europe have come Grauballe man and other millenia-old human mummies so remarkably preserved that flesh and muscle, hair, even facial expressions appear almost lifelike. Recently, at a dig in a Florida bog near Disney World, more than a hundred human burial sites were unearthed, all dating to 7,000 or 8,000 years ago. The most remarkable aspect of this find was the frequent occurrence of desiccated human brains still sealed in their cranial vaults — organs so well preserved that they've provided genetic scientists with the most ancient samples of human DNA known.

Undeniably remarkable.

But even more intriguing — to my wildlife-oriented way of thinking, at least — are the moose-sized fossil remains of a long-extinct species of European deer, the Irish elk, unearthed from peat bogs in Ireland, with fossils of related species subsequently discovered in bog sites in England, Germany, and other temperate areas of continental Eurasia.

Humans can be not just predators but also friends and protectors of wildlife and its habitat.

1

The Irish elk *(Megaloceros giganteus)* weighed around 1,500 pounds and carried outsized antlers weighing up to 95 pounds a pair and measuring as much as 14 feet across. That's a spread of 168 inches. The greatest spread on record for modern elk is a comparatively humble 63½ inches; for moose, 81½ inches—though in body size and weight the Irish elk was no larger than today's Alaska-Yukon moose *(Alces alces gigas)*.

Those dimensions make the headgear of the Irish elk by far the largest ever worn by any creature living or extinct. No matter that the Irish elk technically was no elk at all but an early relative of today's fallow deer (genus *Dama)* and was Irish only insofar as Irish peat bogs have yielded the preponderance of remains of the magnificent beasts.

In its heyday, approximately 11,000 to 12,000 years ago, the Irish elk roamed in great herds across the Pleistocene Eurasian grasslands, living and lusting and fighting and reproducing its eccentric genes for a relatively short while, then disappearing forever. Since stone-age man coexisted with the Irish elk in its final days during the late glacial period—a period of rapid environmental change and general hard times all around—it's not unreasonable to deduce that human activity, in particular subsistence hunting, at least to some small degree hastened the great stag's extinction.

Extinction is forever, and we are left to imagine what it might have felt like to be hiking across the open green countryside of prehistoric Ireland and suddenly encounter a herd of these incredible beasts—their oddly shrill vocalizations alerting us to their presence long before the animals themselves come into sight, their musky scent heavy on the breeze, the broad flat antlers of the mature stags spanning a distance across which a man and a woman could stretch out head to toe. Might we not have savored such an encounter as an experience to cherish? Might we not consider the Irish elk and its pristine habitat a species and a space worth preserving, were it in our power to do so?

Neither I nor wildlife photographer Alan Carey, my friend and partner in the making of this book, have ever or will ever see a living Irish stag. But we have observed and studied, in their native settings, thousands of North American elk.

Alan lives near Missoula, Montana, and travels extensively throughout the northern Rockies, Canada, and Alaska in his camera hunts for wildlife. The remarkable photographs reproduced on the covers and pages of this book are brilliant evidence of his knowledge of and love for his subjects.

I live near the opposite end of the north-south line of the Rockies from Alan and have for many years earned my daily bread (and little more) as a writer and editor. My home and work space is a tiny, self-built, board-and-batten cabin squatting at 8,000 feet in the San Juan Mountains of southwestern Colorado. It's a rare, bleak day indeed when I don't interact with, or at least observe, wild elk—"wild" here meaning animals that roam free on national forest and Bureau of Land Management lands and the sprawling private ranches that border the western public domain, as opposed to those somewhat acculturated elk abiding within the protection of parks and refuges.

When the magic is working, I approach elk up close and unseen in the course of my cautious evening stalks among the conifer and aspen forests that surround my little mountain acreage; I spy on elk through binoculars as they feed and romp and rest morning and evening in the green mountain parks just across the valley; I trade bugles, squeals, and grunts with bull elk during the rut each fall; I contemplate elk in large winter herds yarded up along the cottonwood bottoms of the big river — *El Rio de las Animas Perdidas,* the River of Lost Souls — that flows a few miles west of here; and for a few weeks each year I enter into man's most primitive and intense relationship with elk — I hunt them, my weapons a simple bow and arrows.

Neither Alan Carey nor I want to see the wapiti go the way of the Irish elk. While our continent's herds are healthy, generally well managed and even growing today, and there is little probability of elk being extirpated from the wilds during the remainder of our lives or yours, we hold out the hope that our daughters and sons and their children yet unborn — untold generations of Americans yet to come — will also have the opportunity to experience the magic of elk and the beautiful wild places in which they live.

This book, then, is offered not just to inform and entertain, but in the hope that in some modest way it might help encourage the embracing of a strong and lasting conservation ethic as an integral part of America's national pride.

The extinction of the Irish elk was dictated by the degradation and eventual loss of the biological environment essential to its survival — the oversized, open-country herd beast simply could not evolve into a forest or tundra dweller when the grasslands began to disappear. Stone-age man, while perhaps aiding the extinction of the Irish elk nonetheless is not considered to have been a primary extirpative agent.

As with the great Irish stags, the most significant threat to elk today — indeed, to all wildlife — is habitat degradation and loss. This time around, though, the causes are not natural but rather the long-standing, ongoing, and escalating destruction and usurpation of wildlands via human use and abuse. In the case of elk and other large herbivorous mammals, the habitat pinch is being felt most sharply today in the continued loss of already-critical wintering range.

Fortunately, numerous concerned individuals and groups — such as the Rocky Mountain Elk Foundation — are demonstrating that, even today, humans can be not just predators but also friends and protectors of wildlife and its habitat, thus helping to steady the teetering give-and-take balance between man and beast that nature intended.

Let us enjoy nature and her wonderful diversity of creations now, each of us after his or her own fashion, while striving to leave more to posterity than peat-bog reminders of a far grander past.

Elk In North America
Continental Images

From my mountainside cabin's door, it's little more than a thousand yards aross the valley of our local river to a patchwork of verdant parks and chalk-white aspen groves that make up the big red bull's spring and summer stamping grounds. Where he disappears to during winter I can only guess. Perhaps he wanders the 15 miles and 1,500 vertical feet down and out of the high country to the easier pickings along the sheltered bottoms of the Animas River, as do so many others of his kind. Perhaps he heads the 30 miles or so down to the piñon and juniper wintering grounds south of the town of Bayfield. Or maybe he simply holes up somewhere back in the dark spruce, fir, and pine forests that gird his summertime parks and groves.

I call this particular elk the big red bull for reasons that would be evident were you to see him: that is, his size and the exceptionally sleek auburn hue of his summertime coat. There are other elk to spy on through binoculars as they feed at the cool edges of day in those parks over yonder—sometimes a score or more, most of them cows, calves, and yearling ("spike") bulls. But the big red harem master is far and away the most striking; under the soft morning sun, against the distance-darkened greens of his turf, the big red bull stands out like a ruby in a black man's ear.

This bull, just one of many hereabouts, is a rip-snorting example of why the elk—or *wapiti,* from a Shawnee word meaning white rump (one of the elk's most conspicuous

Wildlife is the exciting element in the landscape. It's like having a stage—a stage with a lovely set. But it comes to life when the actors come on stage. . .the larger birds and mammals make the landscape come alive.
—Wildlife artist ROBERT BATEMEN
(from an interview in Defenders *Magazine)*

Before the arrival of Europeans, elk were the most widely distributed members of the deer family in North America.

CHAPTER ONE

characteristics)—has rightly been called "the monarch of the West." The moose is larger, the grizzly bear more powerful, the mountain lion more mysterious, and the whitetail more graceful, but the bull wapiti, with his proud posture, bugled call to arms, and rich, tricolored pelage (dark brown, almost black head, neck, and lower legs; body reddish in summer and gray in winter; rump cream to buff), is certainly the most regal of North America's great wild creatures. And his crowning glory is a magnificent rack of antlers.

In fact, among elk aficionados, a bull's degree of royalty is determined by the splendor of his antlers: A bull carrying six tines, or points, on each main beam is known as a royal, seven points per side rate imperial status, while those rare few potentates who sport eight or more tines per beam are honored as monarchs. Exactly where on that scale the big red bull falls, I'm afraid I can't say; the distance is too great and my binoculars too small to allow for an accurate point count. It really doesn't matter, though, for he is large of antler, regal of posture, dominant among his peers, a preferred mate among the cows, and magnificent by any reckoning. In short, he is a proud product of evolutionary refinement.

Elk evolved as a distinct species within the deer family (Cervidae) in Asia, then spread westward to Europe as the red deer (stag). Eventually, elk wandered eastward to the

Opposite: Bull in Gibbon River. Yellowstone National Park.
A bull's degree of royalty is determined by the splendor of his antlers.

North American continent, crossing the Bering-Chukchi platform (better known as the Bering Land Bridge), which connected Siberia with Alaska during the Illinoian and Wisconsin glacial stages, beginning perhaps 120,000 years ago.

Some time after elk had become established in what is now Alaska, shifts in climate, glaciation, and vegetation gradually pushed the species out of Alaska, south and east across Canada, and, eventually, down through most of the contiguous United States as far south as northern Mexico. Even though time would eventually render Alaska once again habitable, elk never returned there (on their own) once they left.

While the wapiti was long classified scientifically as *Cervus canadensis,* a species distinct from the European red deer, the two are now considered conspecific and are grouped together under the scientific name once reserved for the red deer alone, *Cervus elaphus.* But this grouping has not been accomplished without dissent.

The two schools of taxonomic thought involved in this ongoing difference of nominal opinion are known in the jargon of wildlife biologists a the "lumpers" and the "splitters." Reasons offered by the lumpers to justify the grouping together of wapiti and red deer under a single species name include evidence that the two probably have been separated for no more than 10,000 years—less than a second's travel across the face of the evolutionary clock—and that they are capable of interbreeding and producing fertile hybrid offspring. The splitters argue that differences in body size (the wapiti is larger than the red deer), coloration, voice, antler size and configuration, geographical loca-

tion, and length of separation are more than sufficient to establish the two as distinct species. Regardless, most wildlife biologists, natural historians, and others interested in such pedantic polemics generally bow to the conclusions expressed in *Elk of North America: Ecology and Management* (the elk-watchers bible). And so shall I.

Before the arrival of Europeans, elk were the most widely distributed members of the deer family in North America. Ernest Thompson Seton, a highly respected turn-of-the-century naturalist with a well-deserved reputation as "the great estimator," employed a variety of methods, primarily mathematical and anecdotal, to arrive at the conclusion that "we are safe . . . in believing that in those early days there may have been 10,000,000 head." Seton's estimate of 10 million elk in North America in pre-Columbian times stands substantially unchallenged today.

In those unspoiled times, the wapiti roamed our continent's pristine forests and plains from the Pacific Coast almost to the Atlantic, and from Canada south as far as Durango and Hidalgo states in Mexico, with one or more of six subspecies inhabiting most of what are now the 48 contiguous states. But rapid human expansion always takes a heavy and equally rapid toll on wildlife, and by the opening of the nineteenth century, the big deer already had been largely eliminated from east of the Mississippi.

On 2 August 1804, Lewis and Clark recorded the first wapiti encounter of their journey, along the present Iowa-Nebraska border near Council Bluffs—an unspecified number of the animals being brought to camp, good and dead, by the party's hunters. By 1922, North America's once-plentiful elk herds had been so ravaged by unregulated hunting and, to a lesser extent, habitat loss, that their numbers had sunk to an all-time low of some 90,000 animals. Thus, taking as accurate Seton's estimate of a pre-Columbian elk population of 10 million, more than 99 percent had been eliminated by shortly after the opening of the twentieth century, the exact statistical fix the grizzly bear is in today.

Yellowstone National Park proved to be the elk's saving space in the lower 48 (as it was also for the bison and is struggling to be now for the grizzly). There, on 3,458 square miles of prime habitat, safe from the greedy jaws of market hunters, real estate developers, and other human predators, a herd estimated in 1925 to contain 17,242 elk prospered. Rocky Mountain elk from the burgeoning Yellowstone herd have since been sown round the continent, which presently supports some 800,000 to 900,000 head.

Close to 700,000 of that total reside in the lower 48, the majority of them roaming free on public lands across the Rocky Mountain states. This is but seven percent of Seton's estimated pre-Columbian population of 10 million, but far and away the greatest number in this century. (Occasionally *too* great for some heavily populated ranges with limited carrying capacities, such as Yellowstone Park in summer and the National Elk Refuge in Jackson Hole, Wyoming, in winter.)

Today there are thriving populations of wild elk in five Canadian provinces; along the Pacific Coast from northern

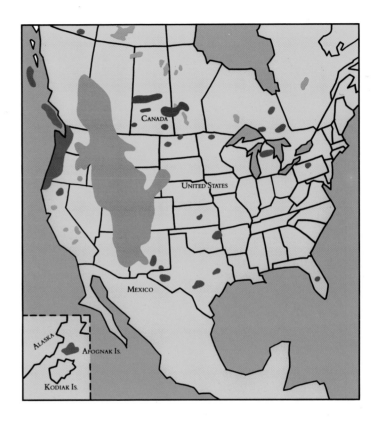

■ *Manitoban*
□ *Tule*
■ *Roosevelt*
▨ *Rocky Mountain*
■ *Rocky Mountain Transplants*

Distribution of elk in North America

California on the south up through Oregon, Washington, and British Columbia; on Afognak and Raspberry islands off the coast of Alaska; in the seven Rocky Mountain states, and the Dakotas. Smaller herds, most of them on preserves, are found in Arkansas, Florida, Michigan, Minnesota, Nebraska, Oklahoma, Pennsylvania, Texas, the Virginias, and Coahuila State, Mexico. Colorado boasts the largest wapiti population of all, estimated by the Colorado Division of Wildlife at around 180,000.

The North American elk, *Cervus elaphus,* comprises four living subspecies, including the Rocky Mountain, Manitoban, Roosevelt's, and Tule races. (Two other races, the Eastern and the Merriam's, have been exterminated within this century.)

The Rocky Mountain elk *(Cervus elaphus nelsoni)* is native to the area from which it takes its name and is the most widespread of the four living subspecies. A mature Rocky Mountain bull, such as my aloof big red neighbor, might stretch to 80 inches nose to rump, stand to around 55 inches at the shoulders, and weigh 700 to 900 pounds (depending on the season) on the hoof—overall, about the size of a small horse. (While a few Rocky Mountain bulls in the half-ton class may still exist, they're as scarce as fur on a fish.) Cows average a couple of hundred pounds lighter.

The Manitoban elk *(C. e. manitobensis)* is native to Canada's Manitoba and eastern Saskatchewan provinces. It carries somewhat smaller antlers, weighs a bit more (males

Yellowstone National Park proved to be the elk's saving space in the lower 48 states.

average 780 pounds, females 600), and is slightly darker in color than its Rocky Mountain relative. There are perhaps 5,000 to 6,000 members of this race alive today.

The Roosevelt's elk *(C. e. rooseveltii)* inhabits our northern Pacific Coast (and thus sometimes is called the Olympic elk) and is the largest of the four North American races, with adult bulls averaging a foot longer and a good hundred pounds heavier than their Rocky Mountain brethren. (A Roosevelt's herd transplanted in 1927 to Alaska's Afognak Island, near Kodiak, has produced bulls in the 1,200-pound range.) Oddly, the big-bodied Roosevelt's antlers, like those of the Manitoban, are smaller than in the Rocky Mountain subspecies. However, due to the occasional occurrence of mild palmations ("crowns") at the tips of the main beams, they may carry more points.

A mere 3,000 or so Tule elk *(C. e. nannodes)* survive today in a few pockets of habitat in central and northern California. (This race was narrowly saved from extinction in the late 1800s at the hands of hunters, ranchers, and settlers through the courageous efforts of rancher-conservationist Henry Miller.) Sometimes called the dwarf elk, the Tule is the smallest of the four North American subspecies, with bulls averaging 550 pounds, cows 400. Even at that, though, the Tule is larger than a caribou.

Those who have seen a bull elk, no matter its race, resplendent in his autumn crown of ivory-tipped antlers, and heard his shrill, eerie music resonating through the still of a mountain night will understand why the wapiti has been called, and indeed is, "the monarch of the West."

Elk And The Indians
Historical Images

Of necessity, prehistoric hunter-gatherer peoples, including early native Americans, were opportunists. That is to say, the pragmatics of survival dictated that primitive human predators take whatever meat happened into range of their spears, atlatls, or bows, fell into their traps, or could be herded into their killing surrounds. They rarely could afford to be picky, and, for untold thousands of years, they weren't.

Eventually, however, most North American Indian cultures refined their hunting strategies — in fact, their entire lifestyles — to concentrate on harvesting a limited number of favored species. When the chosen quarry was plentiful, those animals deemed less desirable were all but ignored. When times were less rich, these specialized hunters still concentrated on their favorite game but were inclined by necessity to take all other edible or otherwise useful beasts that presented themselves as targets.

The quarry of preference for most North American tribes, especially across the vast grasslands of the West and Midwest, was the bison. From this colossal beast, the Indians obtained meat of supreme quality and taste; one bison alone yielded close to half a ton of butchered meat, plus a large, durable hide for clothing and shelter, and bones, hooves, and horns to provide innumerable other items necessary to the everyday lives of nomadic hunters. Native Americans found some use for virtually every part of the bison; little more of the animal was wasted than its dying bellow.

What is man without the beasts? If all the beasts were gone, men would die from a great loneliness of spirit. For whatever happens to the beasts, soon happens to man.
— *UNKNOWN*

In the Midwest and Great Lakes regions, the most striking hints of the wapiti's significance to native peoples are huge earth mounds shaped like bull elk.

CHAPTER TWO

13

Before Spanish invaders brought the horse to North America, Indians hunted bison by stealth — by stalking, waiting in ambush, or driving entire herds of the dull-witted behemoths over cliffs, or "jumps," to their crushing deaths on the talus slopes far below. Later, during the sixteenth and seventeenth centuries, chasing buffalo on horseback became not only a means of earning a living, but a way of life and even something of an art form for numerous Plains Indian tribes.

Natives of the dense eastern hardwood forests, not blessed with huge herds of bison, relied primarily on whitetail deer and a variety of small game animals and birds to satisfy their needs for food and clothing — even though elk roamed the eastern woodlands in abundance in pre-Columbian times.

And so it was that the wapiti was rarely the quarry of first choice for American Indians. But neither, apparently, was the big deer considered significantly inferior or taboo, and in a few areas — such as the American Southwest and the Pacific Northwest — it was, in fact, an essential element in native diets and economies.

Archaeological Clues

How long have native American peoples hunted elk? Two of the oldest known elk-Indian sites in North America are located in Alaska, at Dry Creek and Trail Creek caves, and have been radiocarbon dated to between 8,000 and 11,000 years ago. From these two prehistoric campsites researchers have unearthed weapons and tools of worked stone, along with bits of bone from various large mammals, including

elk. This evidence indicates that elk were killed (or possibly picked up as carrion), butchered, and eaten by the human crafters of the stone tools.

Farther south, in Wyoming, the distinctive conchoidally fluted stone points of the Folsom culture, dating to the last glacial age, have been found in conjunction with sections of elk antler that appear to have been fashioned for use as flint-working tools.

To the east, in the Midwest and Great Lakes regions, the most striking hints of the wapiti's significance to early native peoples are huge earth mounds fashioned in the shapes of various animals, including bull elk. The oldest of these mounds dates to around 3,000 years ago, the most recent to about 800 years ago. Richard E. McCabe, in his exhaustive treatise "Elk and Indians: Historical Values and Perspectives" (in *Elk of North America*) quotes nineteenth-century field researcher S. D. Peet regarding one massive (30 feet by 100 feet) elk mound located in Sauk County, Wisconsin:

[The mound] shows how accurately the effigy-builders were able to imitate the shape of this animal [the elk]. The location of the mound shows that the effigy was placed on the very spot where elk were accustomed to feed, and that effigy-builders were true to nature in every respect.

Such mounds are thought to have served primarily as totems, emblematic of certain clans or religious affiliations.

Additionally, as Peet's mention of the Sauk County mound's location on prehistoric elk feeding grounds suggests, such effigies might also have been intended to solicit the favor of the portrayed animal's spirit.

Native American Methods of Hunting Elk
The techniques employed to capture and kill elk, and the enthusiasm with which they were pursued, varied greatly from region to region and tribe to tribe across North America.

Along the Pacific coast, elk were more often trapped than hunted. One of the most popular and effective traps, especially in what is now central and northern coastal California, was the pitfall. A pitfall consists of a deep excavation camouflaged with a brush lid too flimsy to support the weight of the quarry; when an animal happens onto or is chased over the disguised pit, the lid collapses and drops the unfortunate beast into the void, there to await its end by spear or club when the absentee hunter makes his rounds. Farther north along the Pacific coast, driving elk into heavy entanglement nets was the favored method of capture.

Moving inland to the northern Rockies, in the region of northern Idaho and extreme northwestern Montana, native hunters pursued elk with dogs, set grass and forest fires to scare elk into natural or constructed killing enclosures, ambushed elk from blinds, stalked, and even employed the technique of calling, or "bugling in," bull elk during the fall rut—a caper much in vogue among bowhunters today.

Farther inland, on the western and central plains, before the advent of horses, elk were taken primarily as targets of opportunity and generally by individual hunters, as opposed to the highly organized and closely supervised tribal bison hunts. Thus, preequestrian native elk hunters of the plains often operated much as do modern elk hunters—one on one, stalking alone through the woods or sitting patiently in blinds. On those rare occasions when organized elk hunting was undertaken, a favored technique was to deploy a large number of hunters to surround a herd of the animals, then to gradually tighten the circle until the elk were bunched and could be dispatched with relative ease where they stood or as they attempted to escape through the closing ranks of hunters. Another lucrative native team-hunting technique was to drive elk over jumps, often the same jumps used to massacre bison.

Plains Indians also used traps to take elk, notably pitfalls and deadfalls, the latter consisting of a large log or stone with one end elevated at a steep angle and held up by a trigger set either to release and drop the weight when bumped by the prey animal, or to be tripped remotely, via a pull line, by a concealed hunter.

After the Plains Indians acquired horses (beginning in the 1600s), they became more mobile and bison hunting became even more important, more specialized, and more efficient. As a result, elk were hunted even less than before.

Although the activity apparently was considered unnecessarily risky and so was not a common practice, some Plains Indian tribes occasionally ran elk on horseback, just as they did bison. From Osborne Russell's evocative *Journal of a Trapper: 1834–1843* (Aubrey L. Haines, ed., Bison

Books, 1965), we have a first-person account of these mounted hunts.

> [W]hen the band [of elk] is first located the hunters keep at some distance behind to avoid dispersing them and to frighten them the more a continual noise is kept up by hallooing and shooting over them which causes immediate confusion and collision of the band and the weakest Elk soon begin to drop on the ground exhausted [at which point they are killed by the riders].

In a variation on the same theme, mounted hunters of some Plains tribes would on occasion chase wapiti into lakes or rivers and then shoot the slow-swimming animals from shore, or even swim out and harpoon them with spears or cut their throats with knives.

In the hardwood-forested eastern United States, native elk-hunting techniques paralleled those used to take white-tail deer and included lying in ambush along game trails, herding the animals into natural or fabricated impoundments and then putting them to death, and driving them over jumps. For trapping, the preferred device was a heavy rope snare.

Evidence indicates that native Americans hunted elk as long ago as 11,000 years.

Elk as Food

The average elk yields less than half the weight in butchered meat of the average bison, perhaps 350 pounds, and elk meat is more difficult to store for extended periods without spoiling. Thus, while large quantities of bison meat were routinely dried and otherwise prepared as winter rations — some was dried in the sun, some "jerked" in the smoke of a slow fire, and some was further processed into that wintertime staple of American Indians, pemmican — the majority of elk meat brought in by native hunters was consumed fresh.

To manufacture pemmican, dried or jerked meat was pounded to a pulp, mixed with grease (bear fat was favored) and pulverized berries (often they were chokecherries, pits and all), then packed into rawhide storage containers called parfleches. Properly prepared and stored bison pemmican would last for years (one still-edible stash determined to be around 150 years old was unearthed in Montana not long ago); elk pemmican perhaps for a winter. Pemmican was consumed either straight, much as some people gnaw on snack jerky today, or cut into bite-sized chunks and rehydrated in stews and soups.

The most common Indian cooking techniques for elk and other fresh meat were roasting over flames, broiling in coals, and boiling in metal pots (and, earlier, in skin containers, the water being heated by dropping in red-hot stones).

In the northern Rockies, native hunters pursued elk with dogs, ambushed them from blinds, and even employed the technique of "bugling in" bull elk during the rut.

Nonfood Uses of Elk

The hide of the elk, somewhat surprisingly, is thicker (especially about the neck) than that of the bison, and so is more difficult to tan and work into clothing or shelter coverings, as well as being heavier and more cumbersome to transport. Thus, as with the meat of these two ungulates, elk hides were less popular with native Americans than were the larger, more pliable, and more richly furred skins of the bison. Nonetheless, it's generally believed that elk were hunted more for their hides (and other nonfood parts, such as antlers) than for their meat.

The tough hide of an elk has one special attribute: It provides the most durable leather of any North American wild mammal. Elk skins were highly valued for making hard-use items such as thick rawhide soles for wintertime moccasins and the tough coverings of war shields. (The journals of Lewis and Clark mention braiding strips of green elk hide into heavy ropes, a craft they no doubt picked up from the Indians.) Only rarely were elk skins sewn together to form tipi coverings—too many were required, and such a covering would be too heavy for convenient transport.

The hides of elk and other mammals were usually either tanned or made into rawhide, depending on the intended use. Rawhide is exactly what its name implies—raw, untanned hide. It is hard, stiff, thick, and extremely durable.

To prepare rawhide, a fresh skin first was soaked for several days in a solution of water and wood ashes (or simply staked out in a shallow stream) to loosen the hair. After the

The wapiti was rarely the quarry of first choice for American Indians.

hair was removed by scraping with a hoelike wood, stone, bone, or antler tool, it was stretched in the sun by pegging it to the ground or lacing it to a frame. Over a period of several days, the skin would dry, shrink, and harden, and the preparer had a large slab of rawhide that could be fashioned into innumerable items requiring exceptional toughness and durability.

Tanning a skin was (and is) a bit more complicated. For some uses, the hair was removed before tanning; other times it was left on. After scraping the flesh-side of the hide to remove any clinging fat, the skin was rubbed with a tanning solution often containing the brains and urine of the same animal that yielded the hide. The skin was then "grained" to soften it. Graining involved scraping the meat-side of the hide vigorously with a chisel-like tool, or dragging the hide repeatedly over a large limb or wooden block, much like buffing boots with a shoe-shine cloth.

Finally, hides intended for use as tipi coverings, moccasins, and certain items of outer clothing were smoked to enhance their natural water-resistant qualities.

As with bison, little of an elk was wasted by primitive Indians. Many of the internal organs were either consumed (often raw and steaming, immediately after a kill was made) or saved for other uses, such as the brewing of tanning solutions. Scrapings from antlers, hooves, bones, and hides were boiled together to produce a superb glue; even today "hide glue" (now, of course, made from cattle byproducts) is unsurpassed for certain applications. Antlers and bones were fashioned into ornaments, tools, weapons, saddle frames, and even musical instruments. The long sinew fibers from the legs and back were twisted together to form tough lacing, and strands of lacing joined to make bowstrings, thongs, and ropes.

Mature bull elk have two vestigal canine teeth, commonly referred to as tusks or ivories, located in their upper jaws. These teeth were highly valued as items of trade due to their decorative nature. (In my "animal parts" collection, I have one such tusk; it's a little over an inch long, three-quarters of an inch wide, rounded across the bottom, or biting edge, bent slightly back in the middle, and tapered and flattened at the top, or root end.)

Drilled to accept sinew thread, elk tusks were worn individually as pendants and earrings, strung with beads and other ornaments on necklaces, or sewn—often by the hundreds—onto garments. To the American Indian, the bull elk's canine teeth were the most highly valued parts of the animal.

It was fortunate for the elk that an animistic world view prevented Indians from killing bulls just for their ivories. In later years, the late 1800s through the early 1900s, no such inhibitions would temper the enthusiasm of white market hunters when the value of elk tusks rose to $10 or $20 each and more after they became popular as watch-fob decorations for members of the ironically named Benevolent and Protective Order of Elks.

The Elk in Native Spiritualism
Just as pagan European tribes focused their religious and superstitious beliefs on the natural forces most important to the everyday lives and long-term security of a largely agricultural people, native American hunting-gathering cultures considered the animals they depended on for food, clothing, and shelter as gods of sorts. At the least, all animals were thought to have spirits, and these spirits, both benevolent and malevolent, could be called upon to guide the lives of the hunters and help them through times of difficulty.

In many if not most Plains tribes, it was common for a young man coming of age to venture alone to some distant and perilous place—mountaintops, caves, and cliff ledges were popular—in search of a vision that would shape his spiritual and, to some extent, physical life thereafter. Upon finding a properly cold (or hot), lonely, and uncomfortable place, the supplicant would settle in for several days of fasting, thirsting, and singing, hoping, via his self-imposed privation and misery, to enter into a fatigue-induced trance state and be granted a vision.

Such visions almost always came in the form of the anthropomorphized spirit of an animal or bird. In a typical vision, the spirit, or "guide," would give the supplicant detailed religious instructions and teach him ceremonial songs that could be sung to call up supernatural help in times of great need. Although no particular animal or bird appears to have been dominant in such visions, the bull elk was well represented.

In some tribes, the identity of a warrior's spirit animal was kept a jealously guarded secret for fear that the spirit's help would be withdrawn should its form be revealed. In other tribes, not only was the nature of a warrior's spirit guide advertised (on shields, tipi coverings, and so forth), but special societies, or cults, were formed for men who had seen the same animal during their vision quests. One such cult was the Sioux Elk Society. In his voluminous *Dog Soldiers, Bear Men and Buffalo Women* (Prentice-Hall, 1973), Thomas E. Mails quotes an old Sioux warrior and Elk Society member:

> Two Shields, one of the singers and drummers for this society, stated that the last official meeting of the group was held about 1885. The following song was used by this society, and Two Shields said it had been handed down for many generations. He stated further that the song is still sung by an Elk dreamer at dances and must always be paid for by the man who asks that it be sung.
>
> *Whoever considers themselves beautiful*
> *after seeing me has no heart.*

Because of its great speed and strength, gallantry in rutting battles, regal appearance, and exceptional sexual prowess (a single dominant herd bull sometimes gathers and services more than two dozen cows), the likeness of the bull elk was a popular decorative symbol for medicine bags and other items of import.

The sexual powers of the bull elk seem to have been especially revered by many Indians, the men of some tribes considering headdresses fashioned from elk antlers to be powerful love charms. (A variation of this belief exists today in some Oriental cultures, where the antlers of members of the deer family, especially those taken from elk in velvet, are thought to be potent aphrodisiacs.)

An Unnatural End

As commercial hide hunters, superfluously wealthy European "sportsmen" on safari in the American West, and others (such as the infamous Buffalo Bill Cody) gradually eliminated the bison, the wapiti became ever more important to the red man's survival. But soon the elk too was exterminated across most of its ancient range, falling to the onslaught of white immigration (with its attendant land usurpation, fences, railroads, and graze-gobbling livestock) and, especially, to free-for-all market hunting. (In addition to the uncounted thousands of bull elk killed for their canine teeth, thousands more of both sexes died to provide fresh meat for railroad crews and the mining camps springing up helter-skelter across the Rocky Mountain and Pacific West.)

And so it was that the halcyon millenia of three of North America's most magnificent natives—the bison, the elk, and the Indian—died as one.

"For whatever happens to the beasts,
soon happens to man."

Among The Elk In Rut
Personal Images

It's a pleasant early September evening in the San Juans. I'm out front of my cabin splitting firewood for the perennially approaching Rocky Mountain winter, when an eerie wail comes drifting across the valley, its high, shrill notes knifing in between the rhythmic knocks of my axe. I recognize the sound at once and smile; I'll do no more work this evening. I lean my axe against the slow-growing pile of aspen splits, wipe the grit from my face and ears, and listen.

After a while the wild music comes again—a low, throat-clearing tremolo stretching into a taut alto, wavering up to a soprano vibrato and sustaining, then trailing off rapidly in pitch and volume like a cry carried away on the wind; the finale is a staccato triad of sharp coughs. No mistaking that voice. It's the big red bull heralding the onset of autumn.

The bull elk's time of year, and mine, is here again at last. For the next several weeks, bugling bulls and my sneaking attempt to catch glimpses of them—my own personal spirit-animals—will color my dreams, revitalize my soul, harden my body, and consume more of my thoughts, energy, and time than I can easily justify to anyone who doesn't already understand.

To me, the call of the bull elk is magic. It is one of the most enthralling and mysterious sounds in nature, to my ears equalled only by the chilling nighttime chorus of a wolf pack (a sound seldom heard even in the wildest redoubts

To know the elk is to know the seasons. For it is the seasons, with the grasses and snows they bring, that govern his life.
—DEAN KRAKEL II
(from Season of the Elk)

Conflicts between rutting bulls have evolved to be more symbolic than physical, including profiling, bugling, and minimal-contact sparring.

CHAPTER THREE

23

of the lower 48 these emasculated days). If you were to hear an elk bugle in the night from somewhere nearby without knowing what it was, you'd likely think all the banshees of hell were out there howling in the dark. I'm reminded of a story related in the journals of the early nineteenth-century mountain man Osborne Russell.

While Russell and his little party of trappers and hunters were encamped on Cross Creek, in the Yellowstone country, "a circumstance occurred," he says, "which furnished the subject for a good joke upon our green Irish camp keeper [named Conn]."

The weather was clear and the moon shone brightly about 10 at night when I supposed my comrades fast asleep an Elk blew his shrill whistle within about 100 yards of us. [Russell and his friend Allen pursue the elk under a full moon, but it escapes.] We went back to Camp but our Camp keeper was no where to be found. We searched the bushes high and low ever and anon calling "Conn" but no "Conn" answered at length Allen cruising thro the brush tumbled over a pile of rubbish when lo! Conn was beneath nearly frightened out of his wits "Arrah! an is it you Allen" Said he trembling as if an ague fit was shaking him "but I thought the whole world was full of the spalpeens of savages And where are they gone?"—It was near an hour before we could Satisfy him of his mistake and I dare say his slumbers

Heralding the onset of autumn, a bull elk bugles his eerie call of the wild.

were by no means soft or smooth during the remainder of the night.

An eerie cry it is, but to me lovely beyond description. Other listeners, perhaps less attuned to the music of nature, have commented that the call of the bull elk puts them in mind of a distant rooster's crow, and that the hiccupping coughs often following a bugle resemble a donkey's bray. So be it. For me, the call of the elk is a call to the wilds.

I am drawn to that primal sound as a lonely sailor to a beckoning siren's song. Morning after morning, autumn after autumn, I eagerly abandon the warmth of my bed to plunge into the chill dark depths of the forest, straining to make my movements as imperceptible as the passage of time, as quiet as meditation. Now more than in any other season my senses are alive: eyes prying into shadows, searching for anomalies in contrast and color; ears noting every rustle of leaf; nostrils testing the tangy mountain breezes for the funky barnyard odor that signals when a bull elk in rut is, or recently has been, nearby.

I love this primitive cat-and-mouse game, having at various times slipped up to within breath-holding distance of not only elk, but deer, bears, coyotes. Still, I've never been sneaky enough to run a successful stalk on the big, red bull. He is a far better animal than I. I've stood entranced while he grunted, bugled, and stamped just over the next rise. I've followed his minutes-old spoor and lain in his still-warm day beds. But I have never met the big, red bull up close and personal.

Just as well, for the meeting might kill the mystery.

During the four to six weeks of rut each fall, usually peaking about the third week in September, the bull elk is the horniest of all large mammals. So overwhelming is the monarch's lust that it bloodies his eyes and swells his neck. So agitated is his mood that merely to round up a harem of cows amd mate with each of them is insufficient; the love-drunk bull requires additional outlets for his surging libido — innocent diversions such as antlering brush and saplings to toothpicks, wallowing in mud baths perfumed with his own urine, and bugling incessantly.

Then, too, there's the tension of the challenge. Any bullish elk Casanova who has what it takes to collect a harem of cows must stand ready to prove that he also has the grit to keep them. The cows, having minds and desires of their own, occasionally wander from the fold. Younger bulls, lacking the requisite antlers, muscle, and confidence to openly challenge a harem master, will sulk in the shadows awaiting a chance to spirit away one of the strays for a sneak-thief honeymoon. And mature bulls that consider themselves equal in power and bluff to the master will hoof it in from miles around to challenge the king for his throne.

But since it runs counter to the survival and successful evolution of the species for prime males to kill and mutilate one another, conflicts between rutting bulls have evolved to be more symbolic than physical, including profiling, bugling, antler shaking, bluff charges, minimal-contact sparring, and the like. Still, on the rare occasions when serious physical violence does erupt, it can prove fatal to one or both contestants.

In point of fact: Dr. Gary Wolfe, who, before joining

the Rocky Mountain Elk Foundation, spent 12 years as the wildlife biologist and manager for Vermejo Park Ranch—a large working ranch and hunting and fishing resort in northeastern New Mexico that's home to perhaps 5,000 free-roaming elk—reports that during one recent autumn, ranch hands found the fresh remains of four mature bulls that "conclusive evidence based on postmortem examinations" (broken necks, fractured skulls, antler penetration into the brain, locked antlers) indicated had been killed in rutting battles. Wolfe adds: "If we found four, how many others were mortally wounded and died deep in the woods? Vermejo comprises nearly 500,000 acres, most of it not visible from the roads where our ranch hands usually located the dead bulls. Personally, I believe that combat mortality takes a higher toll than is generally recognized."

Still, most often, bull-to-bull conflicts take the laughably theatrical form of a barroom shoving match between two well-oiled good old boys, neither of whom really cares to have his pretty nose bloodied. Like so. . .

It was late September, and an early snow of a foot or so had whitened the aspen high country on a large private ranch in northwestern Colorado, just below the Wyoming border. A photographer friend and I were watching a large herd of cow elk, tended by a heavy-bodied bull blessed with no great shakes for antlers. The harem master was obviously agitated, blowing off steam with a lot of bugling and being answered, call-for-call, by a subdominant, or "satellite," bull that stamped nervously back and forth atop a low hill a hundred yards distant. Near as we could figure,

the satellite bull was enraged with lust at the sight and scent of so many lovely cows, but hesitant to come down and tangle with the boss. The frustration of this dilemma appeared to be making him crazy.

When eventually the challenger did come down, it was at a run. The harem master rushed forward to greet the threat and *wham!* the two bulls met head-on. A shoving match ensued, the object of which appeared to be to push the opponent backward as fast and far as possible. With the two bulls going at it head to head, it was apparent that the challenger, a royal with a nice spread, was significantly larger of rack than the harem master but outclassed in body size. The "battle" involved very few of the dramatic moves one might expect, such as kicking, fencing, slashing, or clashing together of antlers, but entailed a great deal of locked-antler neck-twisting, snorting, pushing, and pawing.

As I watched the scuffle through binoculars, and my companion through his 400-mm telephoto lens, it became evident that body size and weight count for more than antler mass in such contests—or at least they did in this encounter—with the heavier bull forcing his challenger to give ground in almost every round.

When the upstart finally got the message that he was beaten and had nothing to gain by pushing the matter further, he broke from the fray and scampered like a scolded pup back up the hill down which he had charged proudly only minutes before. The battle of the bulls was done, no

Any bull who has what it takes to collect a harem of cows must stand ready to prove that he also has the grit to keep them.

(visible) blood had been let, the harem master's dominance had been reconfirmed, and both bulls soon returned to their boastful bugling.

Throughout all of this, the cows had remained insouciant, carrying on with their important business of pawing and nosing down through the snow to expose and nip at the still-green grass beneath. This nonchalant behavior in the face of the bulls' boisterous rampaging is not unusual for cow elk during the rut. The females of the species seem to suffer the rut with grace and even a certain dignity and spend their time, when not being herded about or romanced by the monarch of the moment, in normal cow elk fashion —which is to say, grazing morning and evening on grasses and forbs, relaxing in the cool shade to chew meditative cud through midday, and pretending to ignore those wild and crazy guys.

But, in fact, the cows play a far more active role in the rut than meets the eyes of casual observers. To begin with, there's a certain amount of in-fighting and jockeying for social and sexual rank among the cows, with mature females in their sexual prime seeking breeding dominance over the younger and less sexually experienced females. This favors the most fit and experienced breeders, allowing their calves to be born earlier the following spring.

Taking this phenomenon one step further, these early born calves enjoy the double benefit of being reared by experienced mothers and having more time to grow and put

The cows seem to suffer the rut with grace and even a certain dignity, although there is a certain amount of jockeying for social and sexual rank.

on weight before entering their first winter. Thus, what might *appear* to be a simple act of dominance (that is, an older cow pushing ahead of her younger rivals in the breeding queue) is, in fact, a beautifully effective harem trait for helping to ensure the survival of the species.

Additionally, the rut isn't as simple a matter as a dominant bull gathering, holding, and breeding as many cows as possible. True, that's his *goal,* but, as previously mentioned, herd bulls must remain constantly on their guard for escaping cows. The accepted reason for these attempted (and frequently successful) breakouts is that cow elk, in their instinctive drive to assure the continuance (and refinement) of the species, are compelled to mate with the most genetically superior bulls they can find. Thus, if some new bull comes calling with an impressive bugle and antlers that are more striking than those of her present mate, a cow may attempt to switch loyalties.

But evidence is mounting that quantity in mates may be as important to sexually ripe cows as quality. That is to say, not only is a cow driven by instinct to upgrade her mate when an opportunity presents himself, but she may also attempt to mate with several bulls to assure (albeit unconsciously) a successful pregnancy.

For the dominant males, the upshot of these several weeks of relentless rounding-up, holding, defending, and servicing a harem of cows is that many a love-spent bull enters winter malnourished and exhausted—liabilities that can prove fatal should the season prove harsh. For his own sake, a bull would be better off forgetting about the cows and spending his autumn grazing, resting, and putting on weight to assure his survival through the coming winter. But, as with the mating behavior of the cows, what is good for the species isn't always beneficial for the individual. And instinctive behavior in animals is always oriented in favor of the preservation and betterment of the species.

According to U.S. Forest Service wildlife biologist Alan Christensen, "herd bulls lose *considerable* body weight and condition during the rut. Ultimately, this leads them to live shorter lives than the females of the species. [Around 14 years for bulls as opposed to 20 for cows.] If winter comes early, herd bulls can suffer exceptionally high mortality [winterkill], because they haven't had time to gain back any of the body fat and condition they lost during the rut.

"Nature's plan is for the fittest animals to breed both *early and efficiently,* and do so with the least expenditure of energy, thus ensuring time for bulls to recover before winter and for cows to drop their calves early the following spring, giving them the best chance for survival."

Up in British Columbia, wildlife biologist Raymond DeMarchi appears to be making the rut "less chaotic" for the Canadian elk under his purview by managing to protect mature bulls. Older bulls, DeMarchi believes, know the ropes of breeding and so get it done both better and faster, thus accomplishing the natural goals of breeding as early and as efficiently as possible, and doing so with the least expenditure of energy. Conversely, in the lower 48, many of the elk states are taking just the opposite approach by allowing hunting only of four-point and larger bulls, while protecting the immature.

Time will tell.

Three weeks have passed since that evening I was out splitting wood and heard that first bugle of the mating season. The rut is now at its peak, and I'm striding in the predawn chill up a mountain trail I know well enough to travel without a flashlight on all but the darkest of nights. Handy in the big side pockets of my camouflage jacket are a pair of binoculars and a 35-mm camera, both compacts. In a fanny pack and a small day pack I carry the essentials for such an outing: lightweight rain poncho, snack foods, a quart canteen of water, note pad and pencil, first aid kit, maps, compass, and various other emergency and survival items. And, of course, I have my elk call—a small nylon and neoprene disc, or diaphragm, that fits against the roof of the mouth and emits a shrill blast when air is forced out between it and the tongue.

I need an hour and a half to make the three miles from my cabin to the foot of a steep, heavily timbered ridge that rises to an elevation of 9,500 feet. The north-facing slopes below this ridge I know from seasons past to be hangouts for big bulls during the rut. It's still dark when I arrive, so I plant my bones on a downfallen aspen at the edge of a small park to await the arrival of old friend sun.

With the appearance of the morning star in the east comes a bugle, its shrill notes sounding down the slope from somewhere near the ridgetop, several hundred feet above me and maybe a half-mile distant. It doesn't sound much like the big, red bull I'm hoping to meet up with today, but then, I don't sound much like myself first thing in the morning either, and no bull is an exact echo of himself bugle after bugle. It's for me to find out, and I have a plan.

Before a harem master—that is, a dominant bull with

cows—will come to a challenging bugle, the challenger, whether man or elk, must penetrate the old boy's immediate territory. Otherwise, though he may return the challenger's bugles with threats of his own, he's more likely to round up his cows and move away than he is to leave them untended and venture off to investigate a distant boaster, thus risking the loss of part or all of his harem to a third bull while he's gone. The trick in bugling-in bulls, therefore, is to maneuver to within a hundred yards of the bull, closer if possible, without being detected. Then when you bugle, the bull will perceive you as an immediate and proximate threat that must be dealt with and come running. At least, that's the theory.

In practice, sometimes this magic works, sometimes it doesn't. But it's the only game playing in these forested mountains this frosty fall morning. In order to have a chance of meeting this bugling bull up close, I'll have to pull a long uphill stalk to narrow the distance between us sufficiently so that I can hide and try to bugle him in. I gulp down a long swig of water from my canteen and set off.

I make it just a few steps when six big blue grouse flush from close in front of me and flutter ungracefully up to perches on the lower limbs of separate ponderosa pines, just one grouse per tree. There they sit, clucking to one another, stupidly exposed, relying on their elevation and natural camouflage for security, apparently totally ignorant of the visibility of their distinct silhouettes. As soon as I'm gone they'll rejoin on the ground.

Bugling bull elk. Yellowstone National Park, Wyoming.

Farther on, a little dun-colored pine squirrel with a megaphone for a mouth scolds my passing, his ratchetlike curses sounding not unlike a rattlesnake in need of oiling, sounding an alarm call recognized by all forest creatures, including elk. At least the breeze is blowing downslope, as is usual in the mornings and evenings in the mountains. A point in my favor.

Now a second bull bugles, broadcasting from high on the slope I'm switchbacking up, but a few hundred yards off to the west. The bull I'm working on now is above me and a little to the east. I can't go in two directions at once, so I opt to work straight up the slope to just below and more or less midway between the two, from where I may be able to bugle in one or the other. Or both. When the first bull answers the bugle of the second, I pop my diaphragm call into my mouth and, using my cupped hands for a megaphone, offer up my best imitation of a willful wapiti. To my mild surprise and distinct delight, *both* bulls answer. A trilateral frenzy of bugling and counter-bugling and counter-counter-bugling ensues. We're having fun now.

But nothing comes of all the loud talk save for the considerable joys of the experience itself. For most of the remainder of the morning I ascend, traverse, and descend this undulating ridge of steep, thickly timbered slopes, sneaking after what I'm coming to believe must be wood's spirits rather than muscle-and-blood animals.

The upshot of these several weeks of relentless rounding-up, holding, defending, and servicing a harem is that a dominant bull enters winter malnourished and exhausted.

The bugling continues sporadically throughout the morning, but not once do I manage to maneuver close enough to glimpse either of the two vociferous bulls. Nor does my bugling lure either of them to me, though once I do hear a large animal crash away (elk are less than subtle when they move through timber in a hurry) when I step on a dry aspen branch that snaps like a firecracker. But by staying below the animals, the downslope breeze keeps me almost constantly awash in their strong rutting scent—an odor that can in no way be described as pleasant but, given the chance, tends to grow on you.

By noon the breeze dies and the air grows uncomfortably warm for strenuous physical activity, even on these shaded north-facing slopes. My two bulls must feel the same, for they cease bugling. I give up this elk-cum-goose chase and ease downslope, hot, tired, and discouraged. Just as I reach the little park in which I sat to wait for first light this morning, eight elk that have moved in and bedded down during my absence scent-spook and crash off, granting me only a glimpse of their bouncing buff bums in retreat. One of them is a nice bull.

Well.

I rest for a few minutes in the shade of a big shaggy fir, regain a modicum of energy, and decide to hike deeper into the mountains to visit one of my special places hereabouts. Long ago, it had been the site of an outfitter's camp, but has gone unused and forgotten by hunters for many years now; these days, elk bed down and chew cud within the tumble-down remains of what once had been a pole corral for pack horses. Along one edge of this small, grassy, quaking-aspen-shaded cul-de-sac near the head of a small hidden valley, three spring-fed brooks join their modest flows to form the year-round creek that slides down the valley up which I hiked from home this morning.

By the time I arrive, my canteen has long been dry and I'm feeling like a piece of jerky. After dropping my gear in the rich sweet grass, I fall to my knees and drink deep and long from one of the tiny waterfalls that provide this place with its magical music, disdainful in my thirst of that nefarious backcountry threat, giardiasis.

Sated, I splash handfuls of the chill water on my green-painted face, wolf down an orange, a handful of pecans, and a chocolate bar, have another drink, refill my canteen, then stretch out in the flickering shade of the quakies for a few minutes' rest. Not until the cool downslope breezes of late afternoon invade the open front of my thin cotton shirt do I awake.

I sit up and gather my gear. Evening is the second best time of day, after early morning, to interest a rutting bull elk in a bout of spirited bugling, and I've no more time to waste now that I've wasted so much already. But even handfuls of cold creek water splashed onto my face don't shock me out of this sapped feeling; I'm tired from this morning's exertion and sleep-drugged from my stupidly long nap. I don't think I can face the idea of climbing another mountain this day. Not even a small one. Wish I had some camping gear along—maybe a wool blanket and enough food to last another day—but I don't. Oh well, it's downhill all the way home.

As I walk, I'm kept company by the conversation of the little creek chattering cheerfully down its narrow channel a few yards to my right. On either side of the creek and the game trail that parallels it and down which I'm walking, the slopes of this sharply V-shaped valley rise steep and are timbered with ponderosa pine, fir, and blue spruce. In the shade of the trees grow dark purple monk's hoods, light purple elk thistle, and blue-purple showy daisies. Here and there stand groves of quaking aspen. The birds and bears have left a few overripe nuggets on the tangles of wild raspberry bushes along the creek banks and I reach down for them as I go, watchful of the thorny stems.

I am no longer sneaking, but merely walking, headed home. And none too quietly at that. At a point where the slope on the far side of the creek rises abruptly, almost but not quite in a cliff, topping out at the sharp rim of a ridge perhaps a hundred feet above, I am startled by a weird sound, like a strangled horselaugh, shouted down at me. I halt and play my binoculars along the edge of the ridge, but my vision is confused by intervening brush and trees and further hindered by the fading evening light. Well, if I can't see whatever it is, whatever it is most likely can't see me, although it must have heard me stumbling along the trail. I listen but hear nothing more.

On a hopeful hunch I take out my elk call, place it in my mouth and squall out a terse challenge bugle. Immediately the mystery beast atop the ridge answers. It is, as I had suspected and hoped, a bull elk. I scurry beneath the outstretched limbs of a spruce hard against the little creek and bugle again. The bull bugles back, his voice booming down on me at this close range like a 50-amp speaker, hard-edged and crackling with anger. He must be a monster. I can hear him stamping back and forth along the rim, perhaps debating whether or not to come down and deal with me. An apple-sized stone, loosened by the bull's agitated stamping, careens down the slope and splashes into the creek just in front of me.

What, I wonder, is happening here? What brought all of this on? Near as I can figure, the bull was surveying his kingdom from the vantage of the ridgetop, heard my incautious footfalls as I sauntered down the valley, and, unable to see or scent me from his lookout almost directly above, guessed that I might be another elk but was less than totally convinced—which could account for that strangled, half-bugling horselaugh that opened our exchange; he wasn't quite sure whether he wanted to talk to me or not.

I press my tongue against the diaphragm, suck in a deep breath, and insult him further.

For five minutes the bull and I, unseen one by the other, exchange boasts and blasts. But he remains aloof, thrashing furiously at the ridgetop brush and conifer saplings with his antlers, stamping his hooves, but steadfastly refusing to come down to my level. Then the situation changes: After a deep silence of perhaps a minute, the bull bugles once again, the sound striking my ears noticeably diminished, as if he's shouting back over his shoulder as he moves away. Which is probably just what is happening.

I call twice more and get no response, then notice that my hands, cupped around my mouth to form a bugle, are trembling. My entire body is throbbing to an intense adrenaline rush, my physical and mental exhaustion of minutes ago transformed by the excitement of the encounter into anxious energy. I stand, step out from under the cover of the spruce, skip across the creek on a downed log, and all but sprint up the near-vertical slope, unconcerned about all the noise I'm making, for I'm a bull elk just now, and bull elk make quite a racket when they move out.

At the rim, after a long gasping pause to catch my breath, I force out a wimpy bugle. The bull, a wonderfully uncritical fellow, promptly answers. He sounds to have put a good bit of territory between us, and I debate whether or not to follow this late in the day.

I move along the edge of the ridge searching for spoor and find three sets of very fresh tracks, the imprints showing deep and sharp in the sandy soil. Here recently stood a large bull and two cows. (The size of an elk's tracks is no sure way to determine the animal's sex. Better is this: When walking, elk regularly place their hind hooves into the tracks left a moment before by their front hooves. A bull's shoulders are wider than his hips, so the top, or hind-hoove, tracks imprint ever so slightly to the insides of the front tracks; conversely, a cow's hips, built for calving, are wider than her shoulders, causing her hind hooves to imprint toward to the outsides of the tracks left by her front hooves.)

Judging from various bits of evidence, my guess is that this cagey old bull didn't want to risk losing his brace of cows to me (I must be coming on too strong) or was chary of leaving them unattended atop the ridge while he came down to tangle, and so chose flight over fight. The bull's tracks are imprinted over those of the cows, indicating that he's herding them along in front of him.

36   A<small>MONG</small> T<small>HE</small> E<small>LK</small>

I trace the jumble of tracks along the ridge for a ways, then across the top, down a gentle slope, and finally out onto a deeply worn hillside game trail. The trail parallels along above a tight, heavily wooded valley that feeds into the larger valley down which I had been walking when accosted by the bull. This little valley appears to pinch off perhaps a half-mile farther on and is grown up heavily near its bottom in berry brush and ferns. Far below, I hear the faint perking sound of a mountain rill. An inspection of my topographic map shows it to be an unnamed intermittent stream. I dub it Horselaugh Creek. At the valley's head stands a grove of quakies, their leaves autumn-yellow and shimmering in the evening breeze. From here, the straight, chalk-white trunks of the aspens look like so many toothpicks stuck into the earth.

Somewhere down there, beneath that golden canopy and behind that white picket fence of aspen, my bull has halted his retreat and is once again exchanging insults with me, bugle for bugle. But it's becoming too dark to venture farther into this eerie and unfamiliar place this evening, so

I offer a parting bugle, trying to sound tired and defeated — which I am — and turn my back on the most fun I've had in a very long while.

As I trudge home in the growing dark, I think about my day among the elk. This morning the only thing I bugled up was exhaustion, allowing myself to be led uphill and down and all around those steep slopes by two bullish jokers. Conspirators, no doubt. Next I stumbled headlong into a herd of bedded wapiti, of which I saw little more than a flash of antler and a bunch of south ends headed north. Then I wasted most of the afternoon sleeping, and this evening I was outfoxed by the horselaughing bull.

It is said that the secret to being a successful hunter — whether for photos, trophies, meat, or memories — is that you must be smarter than your quarry. Maybe that has been my problem today.

I vow to come back to the little valley of the horselaughing bull. When he and I have both had a few days to rest, I will return.

A satellite male posing a challenge to the dominant bull will do battle for the privilege of mating with a harem cow.

Antlers
Anatomical Images

Why do bull elk possess antlers, and why do the prime breeding males have the biggest and best? It's all part of nature's plan: Antlers are important in establishing the dominance hierarchy and ensuring that the fittest animals do most of the breeding.

— *ALAN G. CHRISTENSEN*
USFS Biologist

In a healthy bull, antler size, weight, and overall aesthetics will continue to increase through yearly cycles of growth and casting until about the tenth year.

In front of me on my desk rest two items of bony headgear once worn by members of the order of hooved, herbivorous mammals known as Artiodactyla (commonly known as ungulates). The first is a small 4×5 antler from an elk. ("Small" here meaning main antler beams measuring 32 inches from burr to tip with the longest of the forward-projecting tines on each beam measuring 9 inches.) The second specimen is a horn from a Hereford cow. The point to be made here is that these two types of cranial appendages—antler and horn—are as different one from the other as are (or were) the animals that grew them.

Although the terms *antler* and *horn* are often used interchangeably, and an argument could be made that in common English usage, such trivial grammatical distinctions don't count for much, it remains that there are significant anatomical differences between the headgear the two words denote.

A mere glance at the specimens on my desk indicates that the most apparent of these differences are in form: A horn is a single, unforked shaft (except in the unique case of pronghorn antelope), widest at the base and tapering gradually to a point at the tip. Frequently, horns are round in cross-section, sometimes oval, and occasionally almost triangular. In some species, such as bighorn sheep, the shaft curls and twists ornately—but it's still a single shaft.

Antlers, on the other hand, are branched, with numerous tines projecting from the main shaft. And while horns are composed of a hard, glossy sheath over a living matrix, antlers are solid (marrowless), dead bone.

While numerous families of ungulates sprout horns, which frequently appear on both sexes, antlers belong to just one family, the deer (Cervidae), and generally appear only on males (a striking exception is the caribou). The antlers of most deer species are round or oval in cross-section, though some cervids, notably caribou and moose, produce antlers that are palmate—that is, broad and flat, resembling massive hands with the fingers spread.

Another difference between horns and antlers is that antlers, like the leaves of hardwood trees, are deciduous— they're dropped and regrown annually—while horns are never shed but are permanent for the life of the wearer. (A single and striking exception to this no-shed rule of horn is the pronghorn antelope, *Antilocapra americana,* whose horns shed their outer sheaths annually but retain the living cores around which new sheaths soon form.)

Further distinctions between antlers and horns are that antlers form as living cartilage that gradually hardens into solid bone, with growth activity taking place at the tips of the main beams and tines, while horns grow from their bases. And unlike antler, horn is composed of Keratin— hard epidermal tissue of the same type that forms hooves, claws, fingernails, and hair. Finally, while horns, no mat-ter their growth stage, are hard and "finished" in appearance,

Through their annual growth sequences, the pedicles gradually lengthen their inner surfaces while shortening on their outer, thus increasing the rack's spread.

developing antlers are soft, somewhat pliable, and covered with a skin of fuzzy living tissue called velvet.

The Miracle of Antler Growth

In all cervids, antler development is timed so that full growth will be attained just prior to the fall mating season, or rut. The timing of the rut, in turn, is controlled (via hormone secretions triggered by the hypothalamus) by photoperiod—the number of hours of light per day.

With elk, the antler cycle begins (or ends, depending on your view of such chicken/egg quandaries) in early spring (the extremes are late January to early May). At this time, the previous season's antlers, now useless and cumbersome to rutted-out bulls, segment just below their enlarged bases (called coronets or burrs), eventually detaching from the pedicles—the two permanent knobs of bone jutting from a male cervid's head. This annual discarding of the previous season's antlers is known as casting.

While both elk genders possess the genetic potential to produce antlers, the male sex hormone testosterone is required to get things growing. Thus, while a rare cow elk will sprout small, soft, deformed cranial appendages known as eo-antlers, it's a decidedly freak occurrence, with normal cow elk remaining bareheaded for life.

In bulls, pedicle development typically begins soon after birth, with initial antler growth commencing at about nine months of age. A bull elk calf's first set of single-beamed, or "spike," antlers will reach maturity, with an average length of 15 inches, by the animal's second autumn, at the age of about 15 months.

For the next several years, each subsequent set of antlers grown by a maturing bull elk will be longer, thicker, and heavier and will usually carry more tines than the pair before. Additionally, through repeated growth-and-casting sequences, the pedicles gradually lengthen on their inner surfaces while foreshortening at their outer edges, thus widening the angle between each succeeding set of antlers and increasing the rack's "spread," or distance between beam tips.

Recent field research on wild Rocky Mountain elk (as opposed to similar but earlier research on captive red deer, the wapiti's slightly smaller European counterpart) indicates that this annual increase in antler size, weight, and overall aesthetics continues in healthy bulls through about the tenth year, then begins to regress. Thus, all other factors affecting antler growth held equal, a bull elk's headgear will be at its most glorious for the four seasons from about 7½ to 10½ years of age. Knowing this, it seems all the more unfortunate that so few wapiti bulls live that long in these times of increasing human pressures and shrinking wildlife habitat. It means that they (and we) are missing the best of nature's promise.

But let's return now to early spring and those raw, bloody skull bumps called pedicles that have recently rid themselves of their previous year's deciduous growth. Soon the wounded pedicle tips—looking not unlike the exposed ends of broken bone—will scab over, providng shields beneath which new velvet tissue wastes no time in forming and pushing upward. Thus, technically, the period during which bull elk are neither wearing nor growing antlers amounts to no more than hours or, at most, a few days per year.

The cells responsible for antler growth are among the fastest-multiplying of any mammalian tissue, generating more than half an inch of new antler length per day at the apex of the growth cycle. Within a couple of months of casting, a mature bull's new main beams will have reached perhaps two feet in length, with the three or more primary tines that project forward from each main beam having attained their full growth of up to a foot or so. By early August the antlers will be fully developed—averaging somewhere around 48 inches in length for mature but sub-prime bulls—and hardened, though still in the velvet.

The time required for start-to-finish antler growth can be as short as 90 days for spikes, gradually increasing with age up to a maximum of 140 days for trophy-class bulls. Since immature bulls tend to begin the antler-growth cycle later in the spring than do older animals, the majority of bulls of all ages attain mature and hardened antlers in loose synchrony during late summer.

I mentioned earlier that antlers grow by way of cartilage deposition at the tips of the main beams and tines. This cartilage is produced by specialized growth cells called osteoblasts, which are sandwiched between the antler and its velvet covering. At the same time cartilage is being added at the tips, it's being replaced farther down the shaft by a soft, fibrous bone matrix that invades from the pedicles and works gradually upward.

If you were to grasp a living antler in velvet and attempt to bend it, you'd observe that the appendage is somewhat flexible and resilient. As the growth cycle continues, the antler gradually hardens, or ossifies, through a process known as mineralization. After bone tissue has replaced cartilage, toward the end of the growth period, calcium and phosphates are absorbed by the porous matrix and gradually solidify (mineralize) to give mature antlers their ivorylike appearance and the hardness of solid, dead bone—which is pretty much what they are.

When the velvet's work is done, its blood supply diminishes and the dying tissue begins to peel away from the antlers in long bloody tatters. Apparently this shedding of the velvet entails some itching or other discomfort, for bulls invariably speed the de-velveting process by rubbing their antlers against brush and saplings, especially pine and other rough-barked conifers. This action not only helps to scrub the loose velvet from the bulls' antlers, but does a dandy job of peeling the bark from the rubbing posts as well. The large vertical scars of these velvet rubs are easily recognizable on small trees and brush and, from late July through early September, occasionally can be found with tatters of velvet littering the ground below or clinging to the rub wound itself. (You have to get there pronto, though, before the nutritious tissue is devoured by rodents and scavenging birds or, occasionally, by the shedding bull himself.)

Left: When the velvet's work is done, its blood supply diminishes and the dying tissue begins to peel away from the antlers in long tatters.

By about mid-October, bull elk are back where they began the previous winter: burdened for several months with 20 pounds or more of useless and cumbersome cranial appendage.

No sooner are a bull's antlers freed from their velvet cases than he enters a rutting fury and commences sparring with everything that will stand for it—brush, saplings, mature trees, the ground, and, inevitably, other bulls. This coats the antlers with plant enzymes that react with oxygen and chemicals within the antler tissue itself to form a dark superficial stain—except at the tips, which are kept buffed to an ivorylike gloss through frequent, and often violent, fencing with abrasive surfaces. (Such tip-rubbing leaves scars on mature aspens and other soft-barked trees in patterns of deep vertical slashes and gouges, as distinguished from the large smooth wounds inflicted on small conifers by velvet rubbing.)

In addition to ridding the bull of bothersome dried velvet, staining and polishing his antlers to look their most impressive for the rut, and serving as an outlet to vent pent-up sexual energy, this scrubbing and honing behavior also enables the bull to "learn" his antlers—that is, to get a sense of how large they are and their exact shape—so that he'll be prepared to maneuver them through thick woods at a dead run, to display them to best advantage to doe-eyed cows and rival bulls, and, if necessary, to wield them effectively in combat. By mid-September and the peak of the rut, the antlers of virtually every mature wapiti bull in North America will be peeled, polished, and ready for action.

After the rut, which typically ends by mid-October, bull elk are back where they began the previous winter—burdened for several months with 20 pounds or more of useless and cumbersome cranial appendage. Eventually, with declining post-rut levels of testosterone, the bond between the pedicles and the bases of the antlers, just below the burrs, will deteriorate until the rack becomes so loosened that any impact or sudden movement of the animal's head will cause one or both of the heavy beams to drop off.

Not always will both antlers detach, on their own, at exactly the same time—a fact that can temporarily leave the half-cast bull with a lopsided outlook on life. I've seen elk attempt to remedy this problem by spearing the tip of the surviving antler into the ground and twisting until the tenacious appendage pops off. Frequent late-winter sightings of "unicorn" spikes, together with the rarity of seeing a mature bull wearing only one antler, lead me to surmise that the substantial weight and bulk of a single large antler is sufficient bother to prompt its owner to work furiously at getting shed of it, while a single puny spike is hardly noticeable to its adolescent wearer, who often simply ignores it until it drops off of its own accord.

And so it is, even as the natural miracle of the wapiti's crowning glory comes full circle, that preparations are already underway for the next go-round.

Elk At Vermejo
Research Images

[W]e crossed the mountains thro. a defile in a west direction and fell on to a small branch of the Galla- tin Here we encamped on a small clear spot and killed the fattest Elk I ever saw. It was a large Buck the fat on his rump meas- ured seven inches thick he had 14 spikes or branches on the left horn and 12 on the right.

— OSBORNE RUSSELL
(from Journal of a Trapper: 1834–1843)

In scoring the aesthetic value of a set of antlers, the lengths of the tines, the lengths and circumferences of the main beams, and the spread between beams are the most important factors.

A bull elk with "14 spikes...on the left horn and 12 on the right"? A prime Rocky Mountain elk these days will carry six points on each main antler beam. That makes Osborne Russell's report of a 12×14 rack seem incredible. But Russell was indisputably credible, "a mature man of high character and good works" who later became the first sworn judge of Oregon Territory. There can be little doubt that his accounting was accurate. Still, Russell was neither a biologist nor a naturalist attuned to notice and report anatomical details, and so failed to observe, or at least to record in his journal, a distinction that would help those of us who are interested today to determine whether the Yellowstone bull in question was in fact the closest thing known in recorded history to the giant Irish elk, or merely an anomaly.

That missing detail in Russell's account is this: Were those many-pointed antlers typical or atypical? That is, were they normally formed and more or less symmetrical be- tween sides, or were they mutant, with many of the tines being small and deformed, the products of freak genetic factors or injury during the growth phase?

I put this pedantic quandary to Dr. Philip L. Wright, professor emeritus of zoology at the University of Mon- tana and chairman emeritus of the Records Committee of the Boone and Crocket Club (the oldest and largest of the two U.S. organizations that score and rank big game trophies, the other being the Pope and Young Club). Dr. Wright's opinion is that a 12×14 typical rack most certainly could have occurred in Yellowstone a century and a half ago, though he doesn't discount the possibility that Russell's bull was simply a freak. (With 26 total points, it would still stand apart today; one of the largest atypical elk racks currently on record was taken in 1974 in New Mexico and has six typical points on each beam plus seven atypical points, for a total of a "mere" 19.) Either way, Russell's Yellowstone bull would have been, still would be, something to see.

The current published Boone and Crockett record for the greatest number of points on a *typical* elk rack is 9×8. But the number of tines is not used in scoring the aesthetic value of a set of antlers, per se; the *lengths* of the tines figure in, but not their number. Other considerations include the lengths and circumferences of the main beams and the spread between beams.

The wapiti rack considered by the Boone and Crockett Club to be the overall grandest in existence is a massive 8×7 typical, taken by a hunter named John Plute back in 1899 at a place called Dark Canyon, near Crested Butte, Colorado. I've seen and contemplated this beautifully preserved trophy on several occasions and judge it to be one of nature's greatest sculptures. The right beam measures 55⅝ inches in length, the left 59⅝; the spread between beams is 45½ inches, and the circumference of the largest beam (measured at the slimmest point between the first and second tines) is a whopping 12⅛ inches. No wonder elk instinctively hold their heads high when on the run: to position their antlers in horizontal profile close along their backs, thus minimizing the amount of forest that gets clear-cut as they bulldoze along.

Any serious admirer of elk antlers eventually comes to wonder what, exactly, are the factors that figure in the making of a monarch? Why might a 12×14 typical rack (although we don't know that Russell's bull was a typical, it's nonetheless fun to hypothesize) have occurred 150 years ago and not since (if one has, it hasn't found its way to the public eye or the record books), and why does the Dark Canyon trophy still stand as the world record when thousands of trophy-quality elk antlers have been measured since its taking? Was there some positive growth factor at work in the past that's missing today? Or is some negative force in play now that was unknown in centuries past?

Until recently, little research had been done on antler growth in wild North American elk; most of the information that has been published, even in the most respected journals and texts, derives primarily from studies of antler growth in captive red deer, the European cousin of the wapiti, or is generalized from research on antler growth in whitetail deer. In that light, the statistics and deductions presented in the following paragraphs are ground-breaking, since they were compiled during a recent 12-year study of wild North American elk.

It is generally accepted that four distinct but interrelated facts bear on antler growth and size: genetics, nutrition, health, and age . . . . Today, modern hunters with their far greater numbers and vastly more efficient weapons take the majority of bull elk before the animals have a chance to reach their prime.

The study was carried out by Dr. Gary Wolfe, who, from 1974 to 1986, was wildlife manager and biologist for the sprawling Vermejo Park Ranch near Raton, New Mexico (with a small corner of the property protruding north across the Colorado border).

Vermejo Park is home to an exceptionally healthy herd of 4,000 to 6,000 wild Rocky Mountain elk (constituting some 20 percent of the wapiti population of the entire state of New Mexico). The ranch is *not* a game farm, and there are no fences or other barriers restricting the animals' freedom to enter and leave the property as they please.

Since Vermejo Park hosts a relatively small number of paying hunters each fall, Wolfe was provided with a wildlife biologist's dream: a long-term opportunity to observe and study large numbers of wild elk on the hoof, as well as a chance to examine and take measurements from those animals killed by hunters.

It's generally accepted that four distinct but interrelated factors bear on antler growth and size in elk and other cervids: genetics, nutrition, health, and age.

Genetics. In order to produce large antlers, an animal must be born with the genetic potential to do so. No matter how well fed and healthy a bull may be, or how long he lives, he'll never grow an eye-popping rack if his genes don't carry the potential.

Nutrition. Being deprived of essential nutrients as a calf can stunt the growth of a bull's antlers for life, even if adequate nutrition is available in later years. And even a large, healthy, and previously well-nourished cervid will produce inferior antlers in times of starvation.

Health. If a bull falls sick or is injured during the antler-growing months, the energy and nutrients required for healing will, in effect, be robbed from the developing antlers and thus retard growth during that cycle.

Age. If the first three growth factors—genetics, nutrition, and health—are adequate, each succeeding set of antlers grown by a maturing bull will carry more tines and be larger than the previous year's growth. But in order for an elk's antlers to attain their maximum potential size within the constraints of genetics, nutrition, and health, the bull must survive at least to middle age.

Since longevity is the factor most severely impacted by human activities and at the same time the most easily controlled through management (that is, by manipulating the amount and type of hunting allowed), Wolfe focused his studies primarily on determining the nature of the relationship between elk age and antler size. The ages of the animals Wolfe examined were determined by dental cross-section, using a microscope to make an annual growth-ring count similar to that employed to determine the ages of trees.

Since elk are born in the spring and the animals Wolfe examined were killed during the fall, their ages are listed in his study in full and half years. The youngest bulls Wolfe examined were 2½ years of age; the oldest 14½, which is approaching a bull elk's maximum natural life expectancy. The antler measurements Wolfe recorded included weight, length, circumference, and number of tines. The data presented below are based on standardized examinations of 482 bull elk.

Antler Points. In general, the younger a group of bulls,

the more the point-count varied between individuals, with older animals showing much greater conformity. The 2½-year-olds Wolfe examined ranged from 4×2s to 6×6s, with 43 percent being 4×4s and 5×4s.

Among 3½-year-olds, 51 percent were 5×5s, with 34 percent carrying more than 10 total points. Of the 4½-year-olds examined, 51 percent were 6×6s or larger; 5½-year-olds, 68 percent; 6½-year-olds, 76 percent; 7½-year-olds, 87 percent; with 100 percent of bulls aged 8½ years being 6×6s or larger. After 8½ years, the percentage of 6×6 or larger racks began to *decrease.*

Writing in the Fall 1984 issue of *Bugle: The Quarterly Journal of the Rocky Mountain Elk Foundation,* Wolfe summarized his findings on age as it bears on the number of antler points.

There is no reliable relationship between age and the number of antler points, with the exception that virtually all spike bulls are yearlings and approximately 90 percent of the 4×4 bulls are 2½-year-olds. Six-by-six bulls are usually at least 4½ years old, although some may be as young as 2½. The average number of antler points per animal was greatest for the 7½-year-old bulls (12.5), but remained fairly stable from 7½ to 11½ years old.

Antler Weight. In contrast to the tenuous relationship between a bull's age and the number of points his antlers carry, Wolfe states that "a linear relationship exists between age and antler weight from 2½ to 10½ years of age."

The weights cited in Wolfe's study include the two antlers plus a connecting section of skull cap, and range from an average of 6.1 pounds for 2½-year-olds to 22.3 pounds for bulls aged 10½ years. As with the number of points, antler weight declined somewhat in elderly bulls, with 17.3 pounds being the average weight for specimens taken from elk aged 11½ years and older.

Antler Length. Wolfe found that the average length of the main beams of the 482 antler sets he measured increased from 27 inches for 2½-year-olds to 51.2 inches for 10½-year-olds, then declined in older bulls. His summary: "A linear relationship also exists between age and antler length from 2½ to 10½ years of age."

Antler Circumference. The average circumference of the 2½-year-olds' antlers was six inches, increasing to 9.6 inches for animals aged 10½ years; the antler circumferences of bulls aged 11½ and older evidenced retrograde growth, averaging nine inches. Here again we see a linear relationship between antler size and age from 2½ to 10½ years.

From the results of Wolfe's research we can reliably deduce the following general parameters concerning antler size and age in wild Rocky Mountain elk: (1) A healthy bull's antlers will be at their prime when the animal is 7½ to 10½ years old, beyond which age all aspects of size will become increasingly retrograde; and (2) antler weight, length, and circumference all increase in direct linear proportion to age between 2½ and 10½ years, while the number of tines is far less predictable by age.

Returning now to the hypothetical question posed at the beginning of this discussion—why might more elk have

produced larger antlers in past centuries than they do today—the answer, in light of the research findings just outlined, is that modern hunters with their far greater numbers and vastly more efficient weapons kill the majority of bull elk before the animals have a chance to reach their prime.

The Vermejo Park herd contains far more trophy-class bulls than do public-lands herds because management there is well-funded, intense, and free of political influence, the habitat is ideal, and hunting is limited and manipulated to attain the goals set by the ranch's wildlife manager.

The fact to be faced squarely and dealt with head-on by all friends of the elk, hunters and non, is that while hunting in general is an effective and even essential tool for the management of elk *numbers,* over-harvesting of spikes by hunters is the single most significant detriment to the production of a larger number of trophy-class bulls.

But, then, just how important *are* trophy bulls in the big picture? While that's a decision to be made by the public and game managers in each of the elk states and provinces, still, it's certain that big bulls are in great favor with hunters, wildlife photographers, and the general viewing public.

Since 1986, Colorado has managed its elk resource to increase the number of mid-sized bulls. This is being accomplished by making it illegal for hunters to take any animal having less than four points on one antler beam. This law will protect young bulls for their first 2½ years

High harvest rates on bulls cause sex and age imbalances in the herd, meaning that natural selection doesn't have a chance to operate.

or so, producing more four-pointers in the coming years—but it simultaneously puts a great deal more hunting pressure on mature animals.

Commenting on this management dilemma, USFS wildlife biologist Alan Christensen (recipient of the Montana Wildlife Federation's Conservation Professional Award for 1987) says: "At issue, really, is the long-term health and stability of elk populations that contain few or no mature bulls (that is, bulls of 4½ years of age and older). A population with mostly young bulls doing the breeding can raise some significant concerns among wildlife biologists. Concerns such as: (1) the effect of a prolonged, erratic rut; (2) reduced pregnancy rates among cows; and (3) later calf crops resulting in higher calf mortality."

"My number one concern," says Dr. Gary Wolfe, "is that high harvest rates on bulls cause a sex and age imbalance in the herd, meaning that natural selection doesn't have a chance to operate. We may be influencing long-term population genetics and behavior."

Limiting the overall harvest of bull elk (in all age categories), then, would appear to be one possible way to increase both the quantity and quality of bulls. But such a proscription would be bitter medicine for a society with a hunting tradition as strong as ours, and doubly so for state game management agencies, whose operating funds derive almost exclusively from the sale of hunting licenses and special taxes on hunting equipment. (Fewer hunters mean less funding, and less funding means reduced habitat acquisition and maintenance as well as diminished management and enforcement capabilities.) Also, in some locations, such as just beyond the borders of Yellowstone National Park in the Gardner, Montana, area, a high annual kill is mandatory in order to keep the number of elk in a burgeoning herd pared down to within the carrying capacity of the winter range. Too many elk on a particular wintering area can lead to conflicts with land owners, overgrazing, and eventual mass starvation.

So, how can the bull harvest be limited without severely restricting hunting and, consequently, the control of elk numbers and the funding of elk-management programs? One possible alternative would be to increase the allowable annual take of cows to compensate, at least in part, for restrictions on the killing of bulls. However, even this approach is fraught with potential problems.

Finding a workable long-term solution to the interrelated but often at-odds problems of holding local elk populations within numbers supportable by the available winter habitat, establishing healthy bull-cow ratios, and achieving populations containing adequate numbers of mature breeding bulls won't be easy. But a solution that is in fact a solution is called for if we wish to maximize the quality as well as the quantity of our elk resource.

Among The Elk In Winter
Chilling Images

*Elk do not use winter range mere-
ly to wait out the winter; elk
move on to winter range to increase their odds of surviving the
cold and snow. . . . But, for
many of the same reasons these
areas are valuable to elk, they are
valuable to man.*

— *JOHN HAVILAND*
(from Bugle)

*It is the presence of deep snow, rather
than shifts in temperature, that serves
as the catalyst for the wapiti's
seasonal movements.*

There is no place on earth quite like the National Elk Refuge
at Jackson Hole, Wyoming, in winter. The southern bound-
ary of this 24,700-acre preserve begins at the very edge of
the little resort town of Jackson. During the snow months
—from approximately November through April each year
—the refuge hosts some 7,500 elk from the southern
Yellowstone-Teton herd, the largest and most concentrated
gathering of elk anyone living today or yet to be born is
likely ever to see.

The elk that spend their winters on the National Elk
Refuge have it easy compared with their non-refuge kin.
In addition to the abundant natural forage, the elk are fed
compressed alfalfa pellets by refuge personnel during the
hardest months of winter. (Each animal gets seven to eight
pounds of pellets per day, which adds up to about 30 *tons*
a day for the entire herd, at a cost of around $300,000 per
winter.)

But the elk that winter in Jackson Hole must, of necessity, pay for their care by submitting to various indignities.
The most trying of these occurs as the animals come down
from their summer ranges in Yellowstone and Teton national parks and off the Bridger-Teton National Forest: In
certain areas through which they must pass to reach the
refuge, death by firing squad awaits.

Each year, a wildly fluctuating number of elk (ranging
from a high of over 4,000 some years ago to a low of just

CHAPTER SIX

55

140 in 1986) are killed in special population-control hunts. In some areas during some years, these events have degenerated into sportless slaughters—shooting-gallery fiascos that dishonor the name of hunting but are nonetheless deemed necessary to pare the ever-growing herd down to a size that can be supported by the refuge. Jackson Hole is geared to wintering 7,500 elk; the net annual herd growth—births minus natural mortality—is about 20 percent, and the number of permits issued for each year's population-control hunt is adjusted accordingly.

To stop the hunts and allow the elk to multiply unchecked would be to assure, within a very few seasons, mass starvation and untold suffering and waste, especially among calves. (E. T. Seton's *Lives of Game Animals,* written just after the turn of the century, cites several examples of mass elk starvation in Jackson Hole during the winters prior to the establishment of the refuge.)

The sensitive observer must wonder if there isn't a more natural and less offensive way to keep the elk population in check in the Yellowstone-Teton ecosystem. Some believe there may be, but caution that nothing can be expected to solve the problem overnight. The Yellowstone herd began seriously overpopulating only after wolves were extirpated from the region. A logical step toward a long-term natural solution, therefore, would be to reintroduce wolves to the Yellowstone ecosystem. Just such a move is presently receiving serious consideration and is enjoying lively debate. Wolf reintroduction is supported by groups and individuals having a wide range of interests, and opposed primarily by a relative handful of stockmen who graze sheep and cattle on private and public lands bordering the parks.

Once the brief annual population-control hunts are over and the elk are safe within the refuge, they quickly settle down to the routine of following the feed wagon, lining out behind the slow-moving vehicle and looking, from an elevated view, like a huge dark serpent writhing over the plain of snow. For $7.50 ($3.50 for children), viewers can sit in bundled comfort in an open sleigh pulled by a Belgian draft horse for a 45-minute ride that will take them as near as 50 feet to the feeding lines of winter-tamed wapiti.

At the refuge's Sleigh Ride Visitor Center, you can view a slide show, a film, and exhibits covering the natural history of elk and the story of the birth and growth of the National Elk Refuge.

But beyond the borders of Jackson Hole and a handful of smaller refuges scattered around the country, for elk in winter, the living is anything but easy.

My little mountain acreage sits in a far back corner of an old summer-home subdivision snug against the San Juan National Forest. My place is connected to the blacktop two-lane down in the valley by a half-mile of rutted but passable dirt roads, and thus is far less secluded than I would like during the summer months. But the area quiets down quickly when the winter snows begin to fall, chasing my few summer neighbors down to greener winter pastures and sealing the roads behind them. (On the Western Slope of the Rockies, snowfall is measured in feet, not inches.) From late November to April, the steep drive twisting up to my cabin is no more than a line of white through the forest, upon which even the most brutish ORVs fear to tread.

Romantic, yes, but romance has a way of fading with familiarity. Not only must Carolyn and I snowshoe a quarter of a mile down to the nearest snowplowed road each time we want to go anywhere on wheels during winter, but we must also haul in provisions and haul out all non-burnable trash — on our backs or dragged along behind in a small sled. Rural Rocky Mountain life in winter is tranquil and filled with beauty — but not always easy. Without snowshoes, we wouldn't be able to live as we do.

Elk have no snowshoes, but a few of them stick around with us through the winters just the same. On my ski and snowshoe outings, I find the bathtub-shaped depressions of their bodies in the snow beneath the minimal shelter of the drooping limbs of fir and spruce trees; I find their acornlike pellets (as opposed to their soft, fused spring and summer droppings) resting in little depressions their warmth has melted into the snow; I find quaking aspens, both standing and downed, with their chalk-white bark scarred by the telltale tooth marks of hungry elk; I find the bare spots where elk have pawed down through the snow in hopes of finding something edible preserved beneath; and I glimpse the animals themsleves, always careful to keep my distance in order to avoid adding to their already significant wintertime worries.

Judging from their tracks, our local elk move about a good deal throughout the winter in their search for sustenance. And they have no snowshoes.

In fact, elk (and deer as well) carry such a high weight loading per square inch of hoof that they commonly sink into soft snow all the way to solid ground, which is sometimes belly deep on a horse. If you've ever tried to posthole your way through a good depth of snow for any distance, then you know well the nasty sort of exertion that type of travel demands.

A couple of illustrative anecdotes. . .

The elk that made it. Directly across the paved county road from where I turn off to come up to my place, a meadow stretches for perhaps a hundred yards to a small river; beyond the river, the ground rears up abruptly to form the far slope of the valley. One morning this past winter, when three feet of fresh snow lay on the land, I 'shoed down to my old Ford 4×4, shoveled it out from under its blanket of white, and drove down to the freshly snowplowed county road. There, looking across the road at the clean white meadow, I noticed a most unusual line of tracks running directly from road to river, paralleling a barbed-wire fence visible only by the dotted line of the tops of its posts. Intrigued, I parked and got out to investigate.

The tracks were fresh, laid down since the county snowplow had made its run-by just before daylight. Descending from the timber on my side of the valley, the tracks crossed first the road and then the meadow before disappearing into the naked cottonwoods along the river. The clear prints in the smooth, plow-shaved snow at the edges of the road showed it was an elk that had crossed.

The animal's trail across the meadow was truly weird, the imprints repeating themselves exactly, as if put down with the aid of a stencil, all the way from road to river —

two postholes in front, two more to the rear, and the huge, pear-shaped imprint of body and neck in between. This elk had literally swum through the snow to cross that meadow and reach the river. He or she had made it, but would have to eat one hell of a lot of brush and bark to regain the calories expended in the effort. And where to from there?

The elk that didn't quite make it. Down the valley a few miles from my mountain, the terrain widens between the road and the river to provide an area of level land vegetated with mixed pine forest and grassy parks covering several hundred acres at an elevation of 7,000 feet. It's ideal wildlife habitat—or used to be.

Until recently, this place was locally famous for the number and size of elk and deer it hosted year-round. Hardly ever could I drive to or from town after dark without seeing several animals near or on the road, crossing on their way from forest to river or vice versa. One night in the early 1980s, I had to brake to a complete stop and sit for five minutes while a herd of several dozen mule deer milled around my truck on the blacktop, taking their good old time in crossing; I reached out the window and touched a couple as they passed.

But no more, for in 1985 the area was transmogrified into a gigantic subdivision (a "master planned community") containing individual homes, condos, apartments, a club-

In general, elk move upslope as the seasons warm, downslope as the seasons chill.

house, restaurant, bar, guardhouse, iron entrance gates, garish spotlighted signs, even a small ridge nominally promoted to the status of "peak" and named by the developer after himself—all designed primarily to attract affluent out-of-state buyers of vacation homes.

The Rockies now have yet more superfluous, over-priced housing and less pristine beauty and wildlife habitat—the very things that have attracted so many nonresidents here in the first place. And, as is too often the case, the planners (and local approvers) of this development failed to provide a corridor of greenspace adequate to allow wildlife to cross safely (that is, a strip of cover sufficient to allow deer and elk to pass unseen by the residents and their predatory pets) in order to visit the river at night for a drink. Since the advent of this boondoggle I have seen exactly zero elk in the area and never more than one or two deer at a time, with those times being rare. This is not my idea of progress, a word suggesting improvement.

But back in the good old days, on a winter's morning in 1982, Carolyn and I were on our way to town when a beautiful 5×6 bull elk bounded across the road 50 yards ahead of us, leapt from the edge of the plowed roadway toward the cover of the pines, and promptly sank spine-deep in the soft snow that had accumulated in a depression a few yards off the road. For all his great size and power, the animal was trapped and helpless.

Elk are in a double bind during winter: They burn a lot more calories, yet there is far less for them to eat, both in quantity and nutritional quality.

I wasn't equipped to extricate the 700-pound bull from its prison of white—no power winch on my truck, no heavy rope, no blanket to toss over his head to lessen the panic—and neither was I certain that I should even try. So I did what I could; as soon as we reached town, I called first the local office of the Colorado Division of Wildlife, then the county sheriff, and got the same reply from both: For various plausible reasons, they just couldn't be running all over the countryside on winter mornings attempting to rescue snow-stranded wildlife. The bull would have to fend for himself. I determined at least to try and help after work.

On the way home that evening we were relieved to see that the bull was gone. Boot tracks were all around the hole where the animal had been, and, from the disturbed snow at the front of the depression, we surmised that some Good Samaritans had tossed a rope over the bull's antlers and, probably with the aid of a truck's power winch, dragged the elk that hadn't quite made it from the snow. We were left to hope the animal survived all the excitement.

I've related these two stories to illustrate the point that elk, especially those individuals that choose or are forced to stay year-round in areas of deep snow, are in a double bind for winter: They burn a lot more calories just keeping warm, getting around, and dealing with the various other stresses of the season, yet, at the same time, there is far less for them to eat, both in quantity and nutritional quality.

How, then, do they make it? To an extent that varies with the severity of the winter and the availability of browse, they live off the dense body fat they've stored between muscle and skin (especially on the rump) during the rich times of spring, summer, and fall. That's why older bulls that lose a great deal of weight during the rut and don't have time to gain it back before the snow begins falling, and calves born too late to put on sufficient weight during their first summer, suffer such heavy mortality during hard winters.

And that's also why good winter range—habitat that's rich in high-quality browse as well as being lower in elevation and receiving less snowfall—is critical to the survival of elk. If all elk were forced to stay on their high summer ranges around the calendar, the species could all but disappear in the course of a single hard winter.

Migration
While the elk's three basic requirements for survival—food, water, and cover—remain the same year around, the daily activities and wanderings of wapiti vary with the seasons. Basically, as the seasons warm, elk move upslope; as the seasons chill, they head back down (although it's more the presence or absence of deep snow, rather than shifts in temperature, that provides the catalyst for the wapiti's seasonal movements).

For countless millenia these seasonal ups and downs were true migrations, frequently quite lengthy. Then we came with our roads and houses and shopping malls and clean farming, all working together to block and amputate ancient wildlife migration routes, leaving the wapiti with very

The National Elk Refuge is host to thousands of elk from November through April.

little room in which to move. (A striking exception is the southern Yellowstone herd, which, even today, annually migrates as far as 65 miles from Yellowstone and Teton national parks to the wintering grounds at Jackson Hole.)

Here in my immediate area of the southern San Juan Mountains, two important elk wintering grounds are down along the hay meadows and cottonwood bottoms of the Animas River valley north and south of Durango, and out in the semiarid piñon and juniper country to the south and west. Both of these ranges lie near 6,500 feet elevation, abound in thermal cover and high-quality winter browse, receive considerably less snowfall than the nearby mountains, and necessitate "migrations" of only 15 to 30 miles or so.

Come spring, the large winter herds break up into smaller groups that begin moving back up toward their summer ranges, following along just below the receding line of melting snow to feed on the freshly exposed sweet new sprouts of grasses and forbs. This upward migration is relaxed and may consume two months or more, with the animals lingering in areas they find particularly to their liking.

My place, at 8,000 feet, is in the midst of just such a transitional zone. Consequently, while a few elk always remain in the immediate area throughout the winter, and quite a few hang around all summer and through the fall (especially

Top: Elk are so heavy that they sink into the snow,
often up to their underbellies.
Bull elk with cow and calf during an early snowfall. Yellowstone
National Park, Wyoming

in dry years), the greatest concentrations pass through in May and June, then gradually thin out as the summer warms and the majority of the animals work their way higher into the mountains.

Elk remain on their cool, green, insect-free, high summer ranges until the first heavy snowfall of winter drives them down. Consequently, the winter migration, as opposed to the relaxed upward drift of springtime, frequently is undertaken as an escape, sudden and hurried. Last year was a good example.

Although it often begins snowing here as early as October, the first really serious storm—a multifoot crusher that closes backcountry roads for the winter and sends the elk loping down and out of the mountains toward their wintering grounds—traditionally arrives within a week or so of Thanksgiving. In 1986, a major storm surprised everyone in mid-October, dropping two feet of heavy, wet snow that stranded (and killed) hunters, knocked out electrical power for 28 hours, and downed shallow-rooted quaking aspen trees by the thousands. (Most quakies had yet to drop their leaves, and so collected large amounts of snow and went down under the intolerable weight.)

A friend was visiting at the time, and since I knew that our local elk favor following a nearby drainage for their downslope wintertime migration, we decided to go have a look.

On snowshoes we crunched up the little valley and marveled at the number of elk tracks we saw there in the new-fallen snow, every last one of the big cowlike prints pointing downslope. The center of the drainage had been so heavily trodden during the night that we found it impossible to figure how many animals had passed. By snowshoeing three miles up the valley and counting the tracks coming in from both sides and joining the main route, we estimated that no less than a hundred elk had passed down this one small valley the previous night, during the height of the storm.

In the coming days and weeks, I returned to that drainage several times. While the lone tracks of occasional stragglers appeared from time to time on the clean slate of subsequent snowfalls, they, too, always pointed downhill. Not a single elk came back up after that first mass exodus. The upward migration that had consumed the better part of two months during spring had been reversed in a single night with the sudden arrival of winter.

Among the Elk In The P-J
Management Images

The three primary concerns for those of us interested in the welfare of elk are . . . habitat, habitat and habitat.

— *JAMES B. RUCH*
Director, Colorado Division
of Wildlife

The piñon-juniper environment is an important wintering ground for elk and deer.

It's an overcast early spring morning, and a mist of wet snow is falling as I trudge down to the plowed road and my truck. Fifteen miles and 30 minutes later, the sun is shining above the Pine Ranger District office of the U. S. Forest Service at Bayfield, Colorado. I'm here to rendezvous with Colorado Division of Wildlife (DOW) District Wildlife Manager Cary Carron and USFS Range Conservationist and Wildlife Manager Ron Klatt.

After coffee, the three of us squeeze into the cluttered cab of Carron's big 4×4 pickup. A scope-sighted rifle and a pump-action shotgun are secured to an "easy rider" rack in the rear window, and a squashed bobcat that Carron picked up from alongside the highway earlier that morning, its right eye bulging out grotesquely, lies in the truck's open bed.

We pull out of Bayfield, drive southeast a few miles then turn onto an unpaved county road streaked with slushy snow. After paralleling for a while up along Spring Creek, we turn north toward Green and Zabel canyons. Between these two wide, gentle canyons rises the flat-topped promontory of Raven Ridge. Off to the east a few miles, their peaks hoary with snow and their high steep slopes bristling with the dark green of conifers, stand the H-D Mountains, a portion of the San Juan Range, named for the H-D Ranch, a British-owned cattle outfit that operated in this area during the late nineteenth century.

Scenario. These two land and wildlife managers have come out here to this piñon and juniper country (they call it "the P-J") today to conduct a field survey of the national forest wintering grounds of some 50 to 150 elk and an untold number of deer (it's difficult to get an exact count of animals that hide or run away). I'm tagging along to see how they operate, perhaps to learn something new about elk and the management of winter habitat, and just to be out and about down here in this "low" (about 6,500 feet elevation) open country after five months of tromping through crotch-deep snow in the mountain forests around my place at 8,000 feet.

Warden Carron parks his truck in a cul-de-sac at road's end, and the three of us pile out and make ready to ascend Raven Ridge and spend the day attempting to determine how goes it with the elk up there in the P-J.

This semiarid piñon and juniper habitat differs significantly from the lush spruce, pine, and aspen forests in which I live, no more than 30 crow-flight miles to the north. Both piñon pine and juniper (genus *Juniperus,* often erroneously called cedar) are squatty evergreens that provide excellent thermal and escape cover for wildlife, and they grow thick on the flat top and steep slopes of Raven Ridge.

The P-J understory is sparse and composed of forbs (in summer), native grasses (now winter-dead), oak brush, some mountain mahogany, and here and there, a yucca plant jutting up like a cluster of small green swords. Excellent feed, all.

The slopes of Raven ridge are steep, rocky, and sandy

of soil. The ridge is surrounded by flat, open valleys, part private land, part in the public domain, and all grown up in sage and its comrades, such as four-wing saltbush. Nearby is a small, dozer-dug watering pond, or "tank" as they're known in the West. As we approach the tank on our walk across the flat to the foot of the ridge, I notice that its banks are waffled with the big prints of elk and the much smaller, heart-shaped tracks of mule deer. Well-worn game trails lead up toward the protective cover of the ridge.

A little farther on, I stumble over an old cow pie, gray and desiccated by wind, weather, and a winter beneath the snow. To confirm the obvious, I ask Ron Klatt, the forest service man, if his outfit leases livestock grazing rights on this land—a controversial and often touchy topic in the arid West, especially for loyal employees of the USFS. He tells me that cattle, but no sheep, are permitted to graze here one month per year, in late spring after the elk have moved out for their migration back up to the high country.

I'm openly critical of the slipshod manner in which public-lands livestock grazing historically has been handled, especially on the 174 million mostly arid acres administered by the Bureau of Land Management. Looking around me now, I see evidence of long-ago overgrazing, possibly as long ago as the days of the H-D Ranch. (Much of what are now eroded sagebrush flats throughout the West were, before the introduction of cattle and sheep, rich grasslands and far less arid than they are today.)

Still, I have to agree with Klatt that sensibly limited

Native grasses and forbs provide forage for grazing elk.

grazing, such as what apparently is being practiced here today, can be a useful tool in the management of certain biomes: In their limited time here, the cattle strip away much of the previous year's dead grasses and other "range litter," thus encouraging new growth; and I see no signs of recent overgrazing or its inevitable eventual consequence—encroaching desertification—just this big gray pile of semi-petrified moo poop at my feet.

Situation. If the cover is adequate, which it is, and water and nutritious natural feed are available, which they are, the three primary requirements for elk survival—food, water, and cover—are satisfied. So why are we here today?

The potential problem in this area is that the national forest lands are bordered by private land, much of it under cultivation, the primary crop being alfalfa (elk candy). Carron and Klatt have determined that the elk are holing up in the P-J on and around Raven Ridge during the days, then trailing down to the alfalfa fields at night to feed on the rich stubble. Although there's plenty of dry grass to graze on, brush to browse, and other nutritional foods on the ridge and in the valleys of the public lands beyond, the animals seem to prefer the stubble left after the alfalfa has been mowed, baled, and trucked away. Carron says this preference results from a phenomenon known as the "fertilization effect," which makes alfalfa, even dead stubble, more palatable to elk than the national forest's dry grasses and browse.

Several landowners are involuntarily hosting the elk, but there have been few problems and only one official complaint has been lodged thus far—a claim filed against the DOW (and paid) for elk damage to a fence. The elk are eating wildflowers up in the high country during the summer months when the alfalfa is growing down here, so there's been no crop damage. Thus far.

Management Goal. Since elk that become habituated to eating alfalfa are all but impossible to break of the habit, Carron and Klatt, as representatives of the two government agencies responsible for the welfare and conduct of the wildlife hereabouts, would like to keep the local wapiti from developing their alfalfa habit any further than they already have.

Under similar circumstances in other areas, elk have balked at leaving their wintering grounds come spring, preferring instead to hang around and become poachers of newly planted crops. The same could happen here at Raven Ridge, possibly resulting in costly damage claims against the DOW, or perhaps even necessitating the "damage control" killing of the offending elk. This occurred just last fall, when a farmer a few dozen miles west of here grew tired of having the public's elk trample and devour his oats, and so demanded either that they be killed or that the DOW pay for the crops they destroyed. The upshot: The landowner was issued a special "kill permit" and he and a DOW warden gunned down eight of the offenders, all cows. Even though the meat was donated to charitable organizations, the public was not happy. Thus, the management challenge here at Raven Ridge is to induce the elk to stay on public lands and off private.

Approach. Klatt and Carron are thinking of recommending some sort of habitat improvements atop Raven Ridge—cover modifications designed to provide more high-quality graze and make the area more attractive to wintering elk—

but so far are undecided as to exactly what action, if any, should be undertaken. The question is this: Will a particular habitat improvement project benefit both the elk and the neighboring landowners sufficiently to justify its cost? At the least, they could simply leave things alone for another season and see what happens; at the extreme, they could bulldoze a road up onto the ridge and bring in crews and equipment sufficient to open up several new "pastures" in the P-J, which would then be planted in forage attractive to wintering elk. A couple of more moderate options lie between these two poles.

Obstacles. One landowner whose property borders the national forest lands—a respected wildlife artist with a background in biology—has made his own survey of the area and determined that a good mix of winter forage presently exists and feels that no intervention is called for. He especially objects to the idea of bulldozing a new road into the area, since this would make access to the rugged ridge too easy for too many people who are too lazy to walk up; he'd just as soon see the animals, the scenery, and the tranquility of the area left undisturbed. Consequently, this landowner has refused to grant an easement across his property, effectively—for now, at least—blocking any habitat-modification projects that would require the construction of a road.

While this man's opinions and concerns are valid, they're weakened by the fact that it's the DOW, not he, who has

The funding of programs to benefit game animals is the Catch-22 of government wildlife management today.

to pay game-damage claims and, occasionally, arrange for unpopular control hunts.

An additional consideration when planning any habitat modification hereabouts is that the regional USFS archaeologist would object to any major, bulldozer-type disruption of the ridge, since such violent activity would disturb and could possibly destroy any archaeological resources that might lie shallow beneath the soft soil. (Pre-Columbian Indian artifacts are common throughout the Southwest and, as standard procedure, any public lands likely to contain them are protected from disruption until they can be examined.) A third obstacle—and it is the *major* obstacle to *all* wildlife management projects—is money: the Colorado DOW, as with most state wildlife management agencies, is severely pinched for bucks.

I beg your indulgence now for a rambling but pertinent aside.

The funding of programs to benefit game animals is the Catch-22 of government wildlife management today. Most of the money spent on wildlife habitat projects on national forest lands in Colorado comes from the national forest system budget, with the DOW typically kicking in only 10 to 20 percent. However, that still leaves the financial responsibility for habitat acquisition and improvements of state-owned lands, as well as wildlife management and enforcement duties on all lands both public and private, entirely to the state agency.

Colorado, as an example typical of most of the United States, contributes virtually nothing of its general tax funds to wildlife programs. This forces the DOW to be a self-supporting entity.

In a typical fiscal year, the DOW receives a token contribution of $1 from the state treasury (earmarked, ironically, for "species conservation work"). Roughly one percent of the division's operating income for the year is donated by the public through a nongame species contribution check-off option on state income tax forms, and tagged to be used exclusively for programs benefiting nongame species. About 15 percent comes from the federal government in the form of Pittman-Robertson (wildlife) and Dingell-Johnson (fish) funds and various small grants.

The Pittman-Robertson (P-R) program—formally titled the Federal Aid in Wildlife Restoration Act—was sponsored by hunters and signed into law by President Roosevelt in 1937. To date, Pittman-Robertson has generated more than $2.3 *billion* (plus considerable interest) for state wildlife recovery and management programs. This has been accomplished through the levy of a manufacturer's excise tax, currently set at 11 percent, on the sale of sporting arms, ammunition, handguns, and bowhunting gear.

Pittman-Robertson money is distributed to state wildlife agencies to help (in the words of a U.S. Fish and Wildlife Service publication) "restore wildlife habitat, conduct needed research, transplant species to areas where conditions favor their revival, and educate hunters in safety and outdoor ethics. Nongame and endangered species are among those which have benefitted."

Another vital service of Pittman-Robertson has been the fostering of professionalism in state wildlife management. This was and is accomplished by placing stringent obligations on the states receiving P-R proceeds. For one, in order to be eligible for these federal funds, states must not divert their own game management and protection funds (raised primarily through the sales of hunting and fishing licenses) to nonwildlife uses. Additionally, in order for a state to receive P-R funds, it must employ wildlife personnel who are trained and competent in their fields, effectively rescuing these important jobs from the political-appointment arena.

Because of the Pittman-Robertson program, America now has hundreds of thousands of acres more wildlife habitat than it would have had otherwise (much of which is also used by the public for nonwildlife-related outdoor recreational activities, such as camping and boating), plus strong impetus for professionalism in state wildlife agencies. And those agencies, though rarely fat and frequently undernourished, now at least, thanks to P-R, have minimum guaranteed operating budgets and are largely free of pressuring or harassment by political caprice.

There can be little doubt that Pittman-Robertson has been the single best thing to happen to wildlife in the history of the white man's occupation of America. Still, by far the biggest chunk of the Colorado DOW's operating budget, (some 80 percent on the average), is raised through the sale of hunting and fishing licenses. The division's single most important income generator is the sale of out-of-state hunting licenses (a nonresident elk tag, for example, currently goes for $250.25). The remaining six percent for the year under discussion came from such diverse sources as fines levied on game-law violators, interest, and donations.

All of this income (around $40 million annually) goes into the state's general fund, then is divvied up and doled out for various DOW programs by the Colorado Joint Budgeting Committee, which, apparently, is how so very many people have gotten the mistaken idea that the Colorado Division of Wildlife and the wildlife agencies of other states are supported by state tax funds. It just isn't so.

Thus, in order to maintain a healthy wildlife management program, state wildlife agencies must sell *a lot* of hunting and fishing licenses. This situation has led to accusations by antihunting factions that such agencies are operating statewide "game farms" for hunters.

Well, yes, sort of—but not in the way the detractors are suggesting. In short, were it not for the money contributed by outdoor recreationists via Pittman-Robertson excise taxes and state hunting and fishing license fees, the American public—not just hunters, but photographers, naturalists, and all stripes of nonconsumptive users of our nation's wildlife resources (including those rare few antihunting activists who actually go afield to view the animals they are attempting to protect)—wouldn't today be enjoying the large numbers of elk, deer, moose, antelope, black bear, wild turkey, and other species that were, at the turn of the century, near extinction but since have been brought back by intelligent "game farming," supported almost exclusively by hunters.

In effect and fact, then, America's hunters are carrying the financial burden of wildlife management for all Americans—including the very antihunters who attack them and their sport. Life is filled with little ironies. Even nongame and endangered species, such as the river otter and the peregrine falcon, benefit from hunter-funded programs in that the habitat purchased with P-R and license funds and managed for game species often is used by a multitude of nonhunted species as well.

As I said in the introduction to this book, there is much wrong with hunting in America today—but there is also much right with hunting in America today, especially as it concerns the funding and implementation of wildlife management programs.

And so it is, no matter what one thinks of the blood sports, that to attack hunting is to threaten the lifeblood of modern wildlife management and, thus, to imperil wildlife itself. It's just one of the many Catch-22s that our overcrowded world must learn to live with.

Between the extremes of serious habitat modification and doing nothing at all to ameliorate the tense situation developing at Raven Ridge, other possibilities being considered by government land and wildlife managers Ron Klatt and Cary Carron include allowing a "Ma and Pa" firewood-cutting operation to come in during the summer

Nongame and endangered species benefit from hunter-funded programs in that habitat purchased with license funds and managed for game species often is used by a multitude of nonhunted species as well.

months with chain saws and a two-ton truck to clear some small areas atop the ridge, hauling off the marketable wood, and burning or simply piling up the limb scraps.

This alternative would cost the DOW nothing and the USFS only some of Klatt's time to supervise the operation; Ma and Pa would make their profit through the sale of the wood (piñon and juniper both are highly valued as stove fuel hereabouts). Trees would be cut and brush cleared on the gentlest slope of the ridge only as necessary to allow them to squeeze their truck through. No bulldozing would be required and nothing recognizable as a road would be established.

An even less intrusive option, though not quite so thrifty as the free services of Ma and Pa, would be to have a two- or three-man woodcutting crew *walk* in to open up a couple of small, experimental clearings, piling up the cut piñon and juniper to provide cover for birds and smaller wildlife.

And so it is that Carron and Klatt are here today—just as other land and wildlife managers are afield in other parts of the country—to monitor the health of this precious little bit of winter habitat. Specific questions to be addressed include: To what degree were available food resources utilized during this just-passed and relatively easy winter (light snow, moderate temperatures)? How much evidence, if any, exists of stress on the elk that wintered here—such as signs of heavy feeding on marginal browse and numerous winter-kills? Finally, if it should be decided that habitat improvements *are* needed, what are the most likely locations for such projects, and which of the approaches to modification outlined above seems most appropriate?

As we strike the foot of the ridge, three big-eared mule deer spook from their day beds in the P-J just above us and bound up the slope, bouncing along in the species' distinctive pogoing running style. The animals appear to be fat and sassy.

The slope here is scarred with the switchback trails of deer and elk. But we humans are too anxious to reach our goal to take the time to reduce the effort of the climb by zigzagging our way up. Deer and elk, being in some ways more intelligent than *Homo saps,* switchback as a matter of course, even when they're in a hurry. But no dilly-dallying for us; we slam straight up the steep grade at what seems to me almost a sprint—it's been a long winter and this is a painful reminder that I haven't been as active as I should have been. (Emerson said it well: "Become first a good animal.") Of necessity, we stop a couple of times to blow for a few seconds and to appreciate the far-reaching beauty of this little corner of the great American Southwest.

We emerge at the south end of the ridge, where the level top is quite narrow, stop to catch our breath, then walk straight across and gaze down upon the valley to the east. Immediately we spot five elk. So bleached are their gray winter coats that the animals appear almost white from this distance. Apparently we've disturbed their morning cud-fest, for they've broken cover from near the bottom of the ridge directly below us and are angling at a trot up an adjacent slope a few hundred yards to the south.

Although no antlers are visible, even through binoculars, one animal is so much larger than the other four and has such a conspicuously dark, heavy mane, that it's certainly a bull. (Some bull elk, especially the older fellows, have already gotten shed of last season's headgear by now, mid-March, and this most likely is one of them.) After a short initial trot, the elk slow, stop, turn to look our way, then trail on up the slope at a more casual pace. (As it will turn out, these five are the only elk we'll spot today—and no small wonder, what with the three of us bashing through the brush, crunching across patches of crusted snow, talking less than quietly, and, no doubt, smelling none too sweet behind all this vigorous exercise. And too, many if not most of the elk that wintered here have already moved out on their slow way back into the mountains.)

We continue on, walking fast, beginning a teardrop circumambulation that will take in maybe four miles of Raven Ridge by the time we're done. The farther north we move, the wider the ridgetop becomes. Although we're walking rapidly, my companions miss little: Here some browsing animal, probably a deer, has nipped the budding growth from the tops of a patch of Gambel oak; over yonder lies a single, disjointed spear of yucca, its edges nibbled (possibly by an elk or deer, but more likely, we deduce from the delicate nature of the chew marks, by some smaller mammal); and everywhere that the grass has greened and pushed up tentative shoots in anticipation of spring, it's been grazed down level with the ground. That's the work of elk.

Farther on, in a tiny clearing, we come upon the withered carcass of a mule deer doe—a hollow package of hide-shrouded bones with bits of dried red meat still clinging to the skeleton. Carron examines the animal's lower jaw—which he finds lying well apart from the rest of the remains, dragged there, no doubt, by some scavenger — and determines from tooth wear that this had been an old lady. We inspect the carcass for signs of a violent or unnatural death but find none. This, clearly, is a winterkill, an animal whose time had come. Winterkills are common and natural — it would be surprising *not* to find them in the spring on any well-populated big-game winter range — and in reasonable number are not indicative of inadequate forage. (We will find only this one deer and no elk today.)

We break for lunch in the midst of a dwarfish P-J forest atop the ridge, parking our butts on the trunk of a fallen juniper — the only dry seat in the house. Our easygoing lunchtime talk suggests that wildlife management means more than a mere secure career in government service to my two companions. Both men are hunters, but neither talks of the elk and deer hereabouts as quarry, nor do they think of their work as game farming. Rather, they speak of the beasts and birds living in their shared area of responsibility as their personal charges — which, I reckon, they are. Our brown bags and juice cans empty, we stash the lunch trash in our day packs, and push on.

After several hours of walking, observing, and comparing notes, we stop to review what we have seen today: High-quality natural forage is available here in abundance but has been only lightly used this winter, and much if not most of that utilization appears to have been by deer rather than by elk. (Deer are browsers of brush and such, while elk's

Habitat and wildlife managers must insure a healthy environment for elk and maintain harmony among all national forest users.

bellies are plumbed primarily for grazing on grasses and forbs.) While the tender, sweet, new spring grass is being grazed with vigor, the dry grasses of last season appear to have been almost totally neglected through the winter. A network of well-used elk trails leads down off the ridge and toward the alfalfa fields on yon side of the valley.

From this evidence, the two managers conclude that there's sufficient food roundabouts to support in good health the number of elk and deer currently wintering here, but, as they had suspected, the elk are selecting the privately owned alfalfa stubble over the public's dry grasses and browse.

It's obvious that no immediate habitat improvement is needed here *to assure the health* of the resident wildlife; the only justification for a modification project would be to provide a greater quantity and variety of natural graze in an effort to induce the elk to eschew the alfalfa, or at least to lessen their dependence on it.

Before any firm decisions are made or actions are recommended, my two companions will need to spend a good deal of time considering the pros and cons of the various alternatives and then consulting with their superiors and other experts. Knowing this, I still press for their initial reactions as we angle back down the ridge toward the road and Carron's truck.

"Based on what we've seen today," I ask, "what sort of action, if any, are you inclined to recommend?"

They remain noncommittal at first, then Ron Klatt opens up. "From what we've seen today and on previous visits, I'll have to concur with the landowner who feels that the wild forage mix is adequate to assure the welfare of the elk, and that no habitat modification is mandatory just now."

"Still," Carron adds, "I'm nervous about these elk using the alfalfa so heavily. While the present landowners enjoy having the animals around and seem perfectly willing to let them graze on their stubble fields in winter, land changes hands so often these days that it's unwise to base any long-term management decisions on an assumption of the continued cooperation of landowners."

"What to do, then?" I press.

Klatt offers that, if anything, he'd consider recommending an experimental vegetative modification offering both minimal impact on the environment and low cost, such as hiring a crew of walk-in woodcutters to open a couple of very small trial grazing areas in the P-J in order to see how, and if, such modification affects elk feeding habits next winter.

Carron concurs, saying that such an experiment would be edifying, would require no road-building, wouldn't disrupt the biological, geological, or archaeological integrity of the ridge, and—if it proved to be even modestly successful in keeping the wayward elk out of the alfalfa—might serve to help convince the reluctant artist-landowner to grant a road easement for larger-scale improvement projects, should they become necessary in the future.

For my part—and my opinion has no influence on DOW and forest service wildlife management decisions (nor am I under the delusion that it should) but enjoys free play here—I'm steadfastly against any additional roading of our country's scant remaining undeveloped public lands, any time, any place, for almost any reason.

Even when roads accessing public lands are gated and kept locked (which recent studies show the forest service to be sadly neglectful of seeing to), backcountry roads, especially *new* backcountry roads, are like magnets for dirt bikers and snowmobilers, who can easily maneuver their cacophonous little machines around locked gates, and do so regularly. And even given the assumption that some future road up the ridge is gated and kept locked and passage around the gate is adequately blocked to motorcycles and snow machines (lots of luck), access into this relatively small elk-wintering area still would be made more attractive to equestrians and pedestrians. And both of these types can get up the ridge easily enough already, if they really want to. In short, an absence of roads does not necessarily mean an absence of access.

In line with that philosophy, and since Raven Ridge isn't a crisis area, I don't feel that any alternative requiring the construction of a road is justifiable. However, a small, low-impact, experimental habitat modification project such as Klatt and Carron are mulling over, while nonessential just now, stands little chance of doing the wildlife or the scenery

any harm and offers sufficient potential for amelioration of what appears to be a developing problem to justify its minimal cost—that is, assuming the forest service is willing to cut loose with the money.

I have recounted this day's events and thoughts in order to illustrate the complexity of the localized dilemmas that must be faced, and the number and difficulty of the decisions that must be made by habitat and wildlife managers throughout North America every day of every year.

As an old Marine Corps buddy was wont to say in the face of adversity, "nothing is easy," especially when you work for the government. I don't envy Cary Carron and Ron Klatt the bureaucratic pressures of their jobs, nor do I agree with them right down the line on everything we've discussed today, nor they with me. (As Montana novelist and conservationist A. B. Guthrie, Jr. has so eloquently put it, "Honest men have the right to disagree.") But I'm glad they're on the job, working for what they feel is best for the wildlife and habitat charged to their care.

It has been an invigorating and thought-provoking day, out here among the elk in the P-J.

Among the Cows And Their Calves
Maternal Images

The cow elk is the one who teaches an elk how to be an elk.
— SCOTT McCORQUODALE
(from "In Praise of Cows," in Bugle)

Because of their larger size, magnificent antlers, and eerie bugling, bull elk commonly receive more attention from wildlife writers and photographers, artists, hunters, and the general outdoor public than do cows. But it's invariably an older cow that leads the herd down to the wintering ground with the first serious snows of winter, dictates the herd's daily routine, and initiates the upward migration come spring. And cows are the sentries, always alert and quick to bark a sharp warning at the first hint of danger.

From E. T. Seton's *Lives of Game Animals:*

There is a widespread idea that the big bull is, as a matter of course, the leader of the Wapiti herd. This is not the case. . . . The individual in that band who can impress on the others that he is the *wise one* — the safe one to follow — eventually becomes the leader. . . . Numberless observations show that this wise one is not the big bull, but almost invariably an *elderly female.* The big bull might drive them, but not lead them. She is the one that has impressed the others with the idea that she is safe to follow — that she will lead into no fool-traps; that she knows the best pastures and the best ways to them; that she has learned the salt-licks, and the watering places that are safe and open all around; that her eyes and ears

The survival of the elk species — as is the case with most mammals — rests in the greatest part with the females.

are keen; and that she will take good care of herself and incidentally of the band.

And, of course, it's the cows that do the hard and dangerous work of bearing and rearing calves. In short, the survival of the species—as is the case with most mammals—rests in the greatest part with the females.

I saw the first local calves of the season this past spring on the evening of 9 June. I was glassing five adult cows as they fed in one of the little parks on the north-facing slope across the valley from my cabin, trying to figure out why these five animals all had completely shed their gray winter overcoats and wore the summer's sleek reddish brown pelage, while a cow and a bull I'd seen up close on my (south-facing) side of the valley only the evening before both were just entering the molting stage. I lowered my binoculars to ponder this little puzzle and to rest my eyes for a moment, and when I brought them back up the calves were there.

Two more cows had entered the park, each with a spindly legged infant in tow. One calf began to nurse the instant its mother halted, standing directly beneath her belly and poking its nose roughly into her udder; in response, Mom twisted her head around to lick her babe as it suckled. The second calf stood and watched its playmate feed, glancing plaintively toward its own mother, who lay ruminating. When the first calf had finished nursing (the average feeding lasts less than a minute), its mother also bedded, leaving the tots to chase one another around the little clearing. After a few minutes of play they tired and plopped down to rest, and totally disappeared from my view in grass and wild-

flowers less than a foot high.

Six days later, on an evening stroll in the neighboring forest, Carolyn walked up to within a few yards of a cow and her newborn calf. The infant, though able to wobble off behind its mother when she eventually fled, was extremely small, had a "wet look," and appeared to be no more than a few hours old, if that.

Springtime in the Rockies, and once again a grand wild species is renewed.

Elk cows are physically capable of breeding during their second autumn, at an age of less than 18 months. In healthy populations with plenty of mature females, however, only about one-third of these adolescent cows will conceive (the ability to ovulate, not the ability or opportunity to breed, is the limiting factor).

If a cow is not bred successfully during her first brief period of estrus, she'll ovulate again three weeks later, and again in another three weeks if necessary—though by then any calf conceived would be born so late the following spring as to seriously endanger its chance of gaining enough weight to survive its first winter (at least in northern regions).

Mature cows in their breeding prime (ages 3½ to 8½) are experienced, know what the rut is all about, and so assert their dominance over younger cows to assure an early mating with the herd bull. Thus, prime cows in a healthy herd generally achieve a pregnancy success rate in excess of 90

Cows are physically capable of breeding during their second autumn, at an age of less than 18 months.

percent; cows on either side of the normal breeding years are less prolific.

The gestation period for elk is 8½ months. Thus, having mated at the height of the rut in mid-September, a cow will come to term in early June. Spontaneous abortions, resorptions, and fetal mummifications can and do occur during elk pregnancy, especially among undernourished or feeble cows. Also, some calves die in the process of being born. Thus, while more than 90 percent of mature cows in a healthy population will become pregnant each year, not all will give birth to living calves.

When a pregnant cow's time approaches — frequently while the herd is lingering in the mid-elevation transition zone that lies between winter and summer ranges — she'll wander away alone in search of a secluded nursery in good cover (oak brush, ferns, and blow-down aspens are sought out in the forest, while heavy sage is often selected in lower, more open country). In addition to cover, a parturient cow will also look for an area that can provide her with food and water without having to travel any great distance. There, in stoic solitude, she will deliver the young — generally just a single calf; only rarely (that is, in 0.5 percent of all conceptions) will she bear twins.

The typical elk babe (Rocky Mountain race) enters the world as a 35-pound package of white-spotted sorrel, though the spots are fewer and less distinct than those of deer fawns. A healthy calf will rise on wobbly legs within

Infant calves will often lie low and motionless in good cover, depending on natural camouflage and a lack of odor for concealment from predators.

Opposite: Typical elk calf.

hours of its birth, will be able to follow its mother almost anywhere she goes within a few days, and by the age of three weeks, will be swift and long-winded enough to escape most predators. Still, the death rate for elk calves during their first weeks—from the elements, accidents, and, especially, predation—is considerable.

Mike Schlegel, a regional wildlife manager for the Idaho Department of Fish and Game, writing in the fall 1985 issue of *Bugle,* summarized the surprising results of a three-year calf predation study conducted in his region of north-central Idaho.

During the three-year period, the mortality rate was 68 percent, of which 64 percent was due to predation. A breakdown of the predator mortality revealed that 73 percent was by black bear, 15 percent by cougar and 12 percent by unknown predators (either bear or cougar).

Even though the predation rate revealed by the Idaho study is abnormally high (especially for black bears) and can't be considered a norm, it points up the significance of natural predators in regulating elk populations and makes it easy to understand how that 90^+ percent pregnancy rate can drop to a nationwide average of around 50 calves per 100 cows within a few weeks of birth. (Managers at the National Elk Refuge at Jackson Hole, Wyoming, figure on a 20 percent net increase in the local elk population from winter to winter, indicating a significant calf mortality rate between birth in the spring and the time the animals reach their wintering

grounds on the refuge.)

With calf predation being such a threat, cow elk have naturally evolved various antipredator strategies. Soon after a cow delivers her calf, she'll devour the placenta and other odoriferous afterbirth that could and often does attract predators. For its part, the newborn will assume a hiding posture, remaining flattened on the ground and motionless except during the several daily periods of nursing. When not feeding or cleaning her calf, the mother will stay at a distance—just within range of vocal communication—so that her strong musky odor won't attract predators to the

Managers at the National Elk Refuge figure on a 20 percent net increase in the local elk population from winter to winter, indicating a significant calf mortality rate between birth in the spring and the time they reach their wintering grounds on the refuge.

area where her calf is hiding. If she becomes nervous about predators, the cow will move her newborn to a fresh location as soon as it can walk, with subsequent moves being made as often thereafter as she deems necessary.

After several days of isolation, the mother will take her calf to join other cow-calf pairs, forming a small "nursery herd" for mutual protection against predators. After six weeks or so, these splinter nursery groups may rejoin the primary herd. There, the adults will continue to surround and protect the young, and the cows will continue to nurse their babes several times daily through about the tenth week, even though the little ones will have begun nibbling at greens after about a month.

Our final calf sighting this year came in early August. We were hiking up a national forest trail, headed for a notoriously elky park at about 11,000 feet. After emerging from a large grove of aspen, the trail dropped down into a meadow grown rich in bunch grass, late-season wildflowers (mostly monk's hoods, showy daisies, and hare bells), berry brush, and scattered patches of runty Gambel oak; along the clearing's bottom edge perked a tree-lined spring-fed creek. As usual, our four-footed Amigo was trotting ahead, several yards in the lead, followed by Carolyn, while I brought up the rear.

As Carolyn approached a knee-high clump of oak brush, a gangly elk calf the size of a small deer jumped up a breath in front of her and raced as sure-footed as a quarter horse down the slope toward the creek. There, just short of the shelter of the trees, perhaps 50 yards from us, the calf stopped, turned just its head and gave us a good long look.

Through binoculars, it appeared to be a young bull.

Carolyn had, quite literally, almost stepped on the calf, which had unwisely chosen to bed down right alongside the trail. His mother was nowhere in sight (though she was almost certainly concealed nearby watching us, her stomach a flutter), and even at the advanced age of perhaps nine weeks, the calf had been employing the "hider" strategy—the name given to the aforementioned instinctive proclivity for infant calves to lie low and motionless in good cover, depending on natural camouflage and a lack of odor for concealment from predators.

The hider strategy obviously worked, even for this older calf, since Carolyn hadn't spotted the animal until it bolted, and Amigo (a sharp-nosed retriever-setter mix) had trotted past within a couple of feet of the calf in its bed and scented nothing. Carolyn's near approach, however, had apparently been too much for the nervous preadolescent, prompting it to break from hiding and run.

Elk mature quickly. By the following spring, that little bull calf will be evicted by its mother to make room for her new charge. Within a year, he'll weigh around 350 pounds and be sporting spike antlers 18 inches long. Another turn of the seasons and he'll be a 500-pound four-pointer ready (though not necessarily able) to gather a harem of cows and mate. A couple of years more (should he live so long) and he'll be an 800-pound, 6×6 herd master like my old friend the big red bull, bugling and running frantically about in an attempt to protect his harem from the relentless challenges of younger rivals.

Oh, careless days of youth, where hath thou so swiftly flown?

Death Among The Elk
Passing Images

There are a great many ways to die, and elk know enough of them.

Wapiti exist in healthy numbers in the wild in North America today only because of the enthusiasm (backed by financial and conservation support) a small percentage of the human population has for elk hunting. It follows, then, that hunting is the leading cause of death among elk. But modern hunting is managed and manipulated to benefit not only the hunters, but, as a species, the hunted. Other killers of elk are not so amenable to control.

Numbering among the many unregulatable ways in which elk die are road-kills (especially troublesome during winter, when the animals come down to roaded and developed areas, lose much of their shyness, and tend to wander onto highways at night in their endless search for sustenance); dogs (in winter, normally docile rural pets, if allowed to run free, frequently will pack up to chase and harass deer and elk; even when the dogs don't catch their prey, the expenditure of calories required to flee through deep snow can weaken an already winter-stressed animal, with death by pneumonia often following); natural accidents and incidents (falls, drownings, avalanches, freezing, and such); predation; entanglement in barbed-wire fences (a special threat to calves); poaching (hang the scum); starvation (a problem only during winter); disease; and everyone's favorite way to go—old age.

The natural world is neither cruel nor fair—those are human conditions.
(from Bugle)

There are many ways to die, and elk know enough of them.

CHAPTER NINE

89

Earlier, I mentioned that death by combat between rutting bulls is generally considered to be exceedingly rare; then I cited the case of New Mexico's Vermejo Park herd. There, during one recent fall, ranch hands found the fresh remains of four bulls that had died in rutting combat—this out of an estimated bull population of two thousand. And since the remains of those four bulls had been spotted from ranch roads, there were no doubt more victims hidden in the vast remote reaches of the 482,000-acre ranch.

The same source, former Vermejo Wildlife Manager Gary Wolfe, also reported occasional elk deaths among the Vermejo Park herd resulting from ingesting toxic locoweed, a notorious killer of cattle and sheep. According to Kevin Lackey, Vermejo's guest manager, "One bite and the elk are addicted. Then they eat the stuff until they die." To hazard something of an oversimplification, locoweed kills by producing lesions on such vital organs as kidneys, liver, and brain. Symptoms include emaciation, trembling, lack of coordination, lethargy, visual impairment, and clear-eyed blindness.

Wolfe says that, of the 13 species of true locoweed in North America, the variety that causes the most problems for elk is the Southwest's *Oxytropis serecia,* or white locoweed. In a five-year study (1977–81) he conducted at Vermejo Park, Wolfe turned up 16 cases of locoweed poisoning (out of a population of 4,000 to 6,000 animals), while in other years there were apparently no locoweed deaths at all.

Combat between rutting bulls may be the cause of more deaths than originally believed.

"Whether or not locoweed becomes a problem for elk," Wolfe says, "depends largely on the availability of succulent forage in spring—which, in turn, depends on soil moisture. Locoweed is not a preferred food for elk. But it greens early, and in drought years it's often the only fresh graze available during early spring. In years when there's plenty of moisture in early spring and, so, a variety of grasses and forbs available, elk won't touch locoweed."

Bearing this out, 14 of the 16 "locoed" elk discovered during the study were found during the two years (out of the five the study covered) receiving the least precipitation.

Additionally, 11 of the 16 locoed elk (69 percent) were aged two years or younger. In a paper prepared by Wolfe and William R. Lance of the Department of Pathology, Colorado State University, which appeared in the *Journal of Range Management* (January 1984), the authors discussed the question of age as it appears to bear on susceptibility to locoweed poisoning in the Vermejo study.

Increased prevalence of locoism in young animals has not been reported in either domestic or wild animals. The significantly higher prevalence of locoweed poisoning in elk [under] 2 years of age may be related to inexperienced forage selection habits of young elk. Additionally, young cervids may finish the winter in poorer physical condition than adults and may have a more urgent physiological need for succulent green vegetation than mature animals.

Summarizing the locoweed situation at Vermejo Park

(from which we can generalize to other areas) Wolfe and Lance say:

> This outbreak of locoweed poisoning coincided with poor range condition exacerbated by subnormal precipitation, and was not considered to be a significant mortality factor in the elk herd. However, locoweed poisoning may significantly affect population dynamics of elk herds restricted to ranges severely infected by locoweed.

Diseases

A variety of diseases attack elk from time to time, but rarely in epizootic proportions. Of viruses, rabies is the only one to which elk are naturally susceptible (as are all mammals). Bacterial diseases, however, are more troublesome. One of the ugliest of these is *Actinomyces bovis,* an infection causing a condition known as "lumpy jaw," an unsightly enlargement of the lower jaw and (less often) other bony structures, with complications sometimes leading to death. Though it does occur in elk, lumpy jaw is far more common in cattle.

Anthrax, another cattle curse, is a deadly disease caused by a bacterium *(Bacillus anthracis)* that breeds in soil and infects livestock when its spores are ingested or inhaled. Wildlife and, on occasion, humans, contract anthrax by frequenting areas currently or recently used by infected livestock. Thankfully, this talented killer occurs only rarely among elk.

A bacterial disease that's neither so rare nor so deadly as anthrax is brucellosis, sometimes called Bang's disease. Wapiti that share rangelands with cattle occasionally contract this ailment, which causes infertility and leads pregnant cows to abort. In humans, brucellosis causes sporadic bouts of headache, chills, and fever.

Rancher Lou Wyman, who raises elk on a large spread in northwestern Colorado, says that all he has to do in order to keep his herd of more than 300 wapiti free of brucellosis is to provide them with plenty of pasture in which to roam and graze (about 1,500 acres), so that they aren't forced to feed over areas they've recently fouled. In winter, when Wyman's snowed-in elk must be fed supplementally, he keeps them healthy by broadcasting alfalfa over a fresh area of clean snow each day.

Internal Parasites

Various parasites, both internal and external, occasionally adopt elk as hosts. The most harmful are the internal organisms, including parasitic protozoa, tapeworms, and roundworms.

One species of roundworm, an arterial parasite, is among the most dangerous of all disease-causing agents to elk, and especially to very young calves. Fortunately, the arterial disease elaeophorosis is limited primarily to the southern ranges of the Rocky Mountain elk subspecies in the lower 48 states, Arizona and New Mexico in particular, and especially the Gila National Forest and Gila Wilderness in southwestern New Mexico and the Apache-Sitgreaves National Forest in southeastern Arizona. There, among summering domestic sheep, elaeophorosis, commonly called "sorehead," has at times run rampant. Several cases

have also been documented at Vermejo Park.

In addition to severe external infections of the face and forehead of its victims, elaeophorosis prompts symptoms similar to those of locoweed poisoning, including lethargy, weight loss, lack of coordination, deformed antlers, and clear-eyed blindness.

The primary host for elaeophorosis is the mule deer, and the transporter of the parasite is the green-headed horsefly *(Hybomitra sonomensis)*. Thus, elaeophorosis can become a significant threat only to those elk sharing a common range with mule deer during the spring horsefly season, and even then, only during years when horseflies are plentiful.

In a normal scenario, the green-headed horsefly takes on the larvae of the parasite by feeding on the blood of an infected mule deer. Later — after the two weeks it takes the larvae to develop into subadult *Elaeophora schneideri* within the fly — it transmits the parasite to the elk on whom it feeds. The most common victims are calves only two or three weeks old.

Once *Elaeophora* invades a host's blood stream, it lodges in the carotid or cerebral arteries, where it continues to grow, often dying and calcifying, eventually obstructing the supply of blood to the victim's brain, and, in effect, bringing on a stroke. After being infected by this arterial roundworm, an elk will die either as a direct result of severe constriction of

Elk are subject to a wide variety of diseases and parasites, but many infections could be avoided simply by providing the animals with adequate nutrition and plenty of acreage on which to roam.

blood flow to the brain, or indirectly by accident, predation, or starvation after being blinded by the disease.

Cattle lungworm *(Dictyocaulus viviparus)* is another common internal parasite of elk. This villain does its dirty work in the trachea, bronchi, and bronchioles of its victims. Inflammation caused by large numbers of lungworms leads to an excessive buildup of fluids in the bronchi and bronchioles, resulting in impaired respiration.

The initial symptom of lungworm infection is coughing, followed in more serious cases by diarrhea, dulled appetite, and increased difficulty in breathing. Death results either directly from asphyxiation, secondarily from pneumonia contracted as a result of the infestation, or indirectly from increased susceptibility to accident and predation due to the animal's severely weakened state.

Cattle lungworm infestation does not, however, mean certain death; many adult elk survive, expelling the mature parasites a couple of months after ingesting them as larvae while feeding on fouled pastures. The primary victims, as always, are calves, especially during their first winter, since lungworms are spread most readily when elk are concentrated on restricted winter ranges.

External Parasites

Nonfatal to elk except in the most extreme cases but nonetheless exceedingly bothersome are a number of external parasites: mites, ticks, lice, mosquitos, and flies. Of that disreputable lot, the most dangerous are scab mites (genus *Psoroptes*), which can cause a condition of massive hair loss known as scabies. Scabies is a "kick 'em while they're down"

infection that selects old, rut-exhausted bulls, as well as cows or calves weakened from disease, starvation, or injury. Since scabies causes the victim's hair to fall out over large portions of the body, it often leads to death by exposure during winter.

Save for the green-headed horsefly, flies in general are nothing but a bother to elk; but, on occasion, they can be such a tremendous bother that they force the besieged animals to roll and cake themselves in mud, to head for the high, wind-swept slopes above timberline, or to act more like water buffalo than wapiti. Concerning this latter caper—elk emersing themselves in water to avoid flies and other stinging insects—E. T. Seton, in his *Lives of Game Animals,* quotes an 1866 anecdote related by one J. K. Lord:

> Travelling in Oregon, one constantly finds oneself on the banks of a wide glassy lake; gazing over its unrippled surface, the eye suddenly rests on what to the inexperienced in the hunter's craft, appears to be small clumps of twisted branches, or dead and leafless tree-tops, the trunks of which are hidden in the water; but the Indian and trapper discerns in a second that the apparent branches are the antlers of a herd of Wapiti that has been driven into the water by Breeze flies *(Tabanus atratus).*

Notwithstanding the foregoing overview of unpleasant diseases and parasites, elk are essentially clean, healthy animals, and would be healthier yet were it not for the plethora of ailments spread to them by domestic livestock.

Many parasites and bacterial infections can be avoided in elk simply by providing the animals with adequate nutrition and plenty of acreage on which to roam, preferably at a safe distance from the recent stamping grounds of cattle and sheep.

The Bull In The Bog
Death by bullet or arrow at the hands of a skilled hunter is clean, quick, and humane. Man has always had a predator-prey relationship with many of his fellow mammals—a natural and healthful relationship when pursued with an ethical attitude and respect for the animal hunted.

What disturbs me is to see wild animals suffer and die uselessly as an indirect result of the frequently careless doings of humans: a calf with both hind legs tangled in a coil of discarded barbed wire and slowly starving, her only hope for relief being quick death at the jaws of predators; a cow elk lying in shock alongside a highway after being struck down by a speeding tractor-trailer rig that couldn't or wouldn't slow for the light-blinded animal; deer and elk starving and freezing in the high country because critical migration routes down to their wintering grounds have been cut off by roads and commercial and residential developments that are planned, approved by local governments, and built with no or inadequate allowance for wildlife corridors.

But, by human reckoning, at least, nature too can be cruel. A compelling example of this is related by photographer Alan Carey, who happened upon and filmed such a tragedy a few years ago.

"It was late October and I was working in the Blacktail Lakes region in the northern part of Yellowstone National Park, looking for river otters to photograph. I spotted a pair of coyotes feeding on something about a quarter of a mile away and, since I'd had no luck finding river otters, figured I might as well try stalking the alert predators. The country was completely open with no cover of any kind, and the odds were slim that I'd get near enough for any decent shots. As it turned out, I didn't even make the first hundred yards before the coyotes spotted me and fled.

"Since I was pointed in that direction, I decided to continue on and investigate what the coyotes had been dining on. As I approached the site, I was amazed to see just the mud-covered head of a small five-point bull elk appearing to be sitting on the ground.

"As I drew closer, I could see that the animal was mired up to his neck in a natural mud bog about 10 feet in diameter. When I moved to within about 10 yards of the elk, he raised his head and looked at me. The pain and fear in his eyes were unmistakable. Just behind him floated the bloody rib cage of another elk that had met a similar fate sometime earlier. These floating bones, apparently, were what the coyotes had been gnawing on.

"I felt a touch of sadness as I watched the elk twist his head back and forth in a feeble and useless effort to free himself from what almost certainly would soon become his muddy tomb.

"I took a few pictures of this gruesome sight, then, reluctantly, prepared to move on. There was nothing I or anyone else could do to help the hapless creature. And even if there

had been, the park service has a policy of letting nature take its course in Yellowstone—a policy which, on occasion, has aroused considerable controversy.

"As I was leaving, I noticed a park ranger walking down a nearby slope, headed my way. When we met, he said that he'd seen me photographing the elk and wondered if the animal was still alive. I answered yes, it was, but barely. The ranger then told me that he'd first noticed the elk stuck in the bog a week before and was surprised that it had survived for so long.

"I wasn't able to return the next day to see if the bull had made it through another night. But it was some time before I could forget the anguish I'd seen in the animal's eyes or shake off my guilt at not having found some way to end his misery quickly, rather than complying with the manmade directive that commanded me to turn my back and walk away from the prolonged suffering of such a grand creature.

"I read recently that nature is neither cruel nor fair, that those are human concepts. It's true, of course—but sometimes you have to wonder."

The bull in the bog.

You Among The Elk
Close-Up Images

"Elk are where you find them."
(often heard in the Rockies)

Yellowstone in September is the place to be to see the largest herd of extant elk at the height of the annual rut.

The most accessible locales for elk watching are Yellowstone (in Wyoming and Montana), Glacier (Montana), and Rocky Mountain (Colorado) national parks, the National Bison Range (Montana), and the National Elk Refuge (at Jackson, Wyoming). Additionally, elk are plentiful—albeit more scattered and considerably more elusive than in the parks and refuges—on many national forest and BLM lands throughout the mountainous regions of Arizona, Colorado, Idaho, Montana, New Mexico, Oregon, Utah, Washington State, and Wyoming.

If I had to recommend one time and one place as the all-around best bet for viewing elk in glorious surroundings, I'd suggest heading for Yellowstone in late September. That will put you in the midst of the largest herd of elk extant (actually, two herds, north and south) at the height of the annual rut. Throughout the sprawling park at this time of year the light takes on a magical quality, the crisp morning air is charged with the excitement of the changing seasons, bulls are competing vocally and physically to gather cows into harems, and the air rings, day and night, with their lustful whistles.

During one fall a few years ago, Carolyn and I were living at Red Lodge, just over Beartooth Pass to the north and east of the park, and so visited there regularly. We quickly became addicted to watching, listening to, and photographing elk at this, their most active, time of the year.

CHAPTER TEN

99

It was in Yellowstone one day in late September that year that I learned a valuable lesson about the behavior of bull elk in rut—and about the behavior of *Homo sapiens* en masse.

While driving slowly along a paved park road in the Lamar Valley area, I spotted a bull thrashing about in a mud wallow at the far edge of a large park, perhaps 300 yards from the road. After checking the old boy out through binoculars and determining that he was a good one, I decided to try for some photographs. Carolyn stayed with the truck while I angled out across the grassy park, indirectly approaching the distracted bull.

I was shooting through a 300-mm lens and figured I needed to maneuver to within a hundred yards of the animal in order to get the shots I wanted. At that distance, I reckoned, I wouldn't be crowding the bull and, if I kept my movements slow and relaxed, I shouldn't alarm him sufficiently to alter his normal behavior. What I hadn't figured on was a phenomenon I've since come to call the Yellowstone Contagion. That is, as soon as a vehicle stops anywhere other than at a designated pullout along a park road, all other passing motorists assume (usually correctly) that the driver of the parked car has spotted an interesting animal, and so they stop too. Within minutes the road was lined with parked cars, and no less than two dozen camera-armed citizens were scurrying toward me and the wallowing bull.

During the snow-free months, elk generally prefer remote areas offering secluded grassy parks surrounded by thick forests of mixed conifers.

He was a magnificent beast, his antlers heavy and carrying six points to the side. The tines were draped with clumps of turf and hung with shreds of vegetation he'd recently abused. His bulky body was covered in urine-soaked mud and his eyes showed blood red through my binoculars. In spite of his size, this obviously was a satellite bull—an animal that, so far, hadn't been able to gather and keep a harem of cows—in this instance perhaps due to advancing age. (Else he would have been with the cows rather than slopping around alone in a mud hole, his legs kicking in the air like some outsized dog scratching his back.) I should have known that he'd be a bit out of sorts and edgy.

I enjoyed five minutes of undisturbed shooting before being joined by the Yellowstone Contagion crowd. Too soon, all manner of unmannered shutterbugs were crowding me and "my" bull. One big grumpy woman toting a Polaroid shouldered roughly past then stopped smack in front of me to take her snapshots; we might as well have been in a crowded department store.

Now I too became infected with this mass idiocy and began moving closer to the bull in an effort to stay out front of the crowd and keep a clear field of vision long enough to finish the 36-exposure roll of film I'd started.

When the mob of photographers, I at its fore, had closed to within about 20 yards of the bull, the poor pestered beast clambered to his feet, drew back his lips to bare his teeth, hissed at us (yes, *hissed*), jerked his head down to present his antlers in a manner most formidable, trotted forward a few yards, stopped, grunted, and stamped the ground. Was he ever hot.

That scattered the crowd, most of whom, myself included, returned forthwith to the safety of their vehicles. Alone again at last, the bull sauntered over to a pine sapling at the edge of the park and commenced shredding it with his ample antlers, no doubt pretending it was me or that rude lady with the Polaroid.

I got some nice shots during that episode, a few of which have since been published in magazines, but I could have gotten myself gored in the doing. The lessons I learned from the bull and the tourists that fall day in Yellowstone Park were two: Know that normally shy elk, even park animals, can, if provoked, react aggressively, especially during the rut; and never crowd elk or other large animals, no matter how insouciant they may appear.

Since moving to Colorado, Carolyn and I have tried to make an annual pilgrimage to the Yellowstone-Teton-Glacier region of the northern rockies, preferably in the fall. Last year, however, we went during early June in order to see and photograph newborn elk calves, and were mildly disappointed.

Wee elk were abundant, but the wapiti, big and small, were in the process of molting their winter coats, most having shabby, moth-eaten pelages. (The Blackfeet Indians referred to animals in this stage of molt as "scabby robes.") Decidedly unphotogenic.

There are, however, certain special attractions awaiting wapiti watchers who visit Yellowstone in the spring. At that time of year, winter-famished elk in the overpopulated (and, in some areas, overgrazed) park are driven by hunger to become particularly bold; many of the campgrounds we

visited had nearly as many wapiti roaming around, grazing on the new green grasses and forbs, as they had human campers. This phenomenon — the remarkable temerity of normally shy refuge and park animals during certain seasons — is a mixed blessing. For those visitors who could or would never stalk the backcountry to spy on truly wild elk, easy access to these desensitized animals is a blessing. Children — and adults who have never before seen an uncaged elk up close — invariably love it.

The down side of this situation is that park and refuge elk, through long association with humans in a protected environment, tend to lose the aloof dignity of their unprotected kin. In the worst of cases, park elk are reduced to behaving more like feedlot Herefords than like the regal and elusive creatures nature intended them to be. Thus, while our western national parks and game refuges are wapiti treasure chests for urban folk and wildlife photographers, those who have viewed the genuine article in genuine wilderness may be a bit disappointed to see a big bull in velvet eating vanilla wafers from the hands of a cherubic 12-year-old.

As with visiting Yellowstone in spring, in winter the National Elk Refuge at Jackson Hole, Wyoming, provides easy access to large numbers of elk for thousands of people who would most likely never see a free-roaming wapiti any other way. However, also akin to the Yellowstone situa-

Park and refuge elk, through long association with humans in a protected environment, tend to lose the aloof dignity of their unprotected kin, although a mother with young is always wary.

tion, the Jackson Hole animals, reduced for the duration of winter to trailing like beggars along behind the grub wagon, can be something of a disappointment to those who are accustomed to observing them under more natural circumstances.

Still, 15,000 jets of breath puffing white from the nostrils of 7,500 elk on a frosty January morning is definitely something to see.

Stalking the Wild Wapiti

If you think you might someday want to try pulling a sneak on the free-roaming elk of our national forests and other public lands — whether as a photographer, hunter, or nature observer — there are a few things to know that will make the experience both easier and more rewarding.

To find wild elk, first travel to an area you know to host a healthy population of the animals (state wildlife agencies and regional offices of the U. S. Forest Service will point you in the right directions). Next, use topographic maps to identify off-the-beaten-path terrain that satisfies all three of the wapiti's basic requirements for survival: food, water, and cover. In general, look for the greatest concentrations of elk at lower elevations during winter, in mid-elevation transition zones during spring and early summer, and in the high country during late summer and fall, until the first heavy snows.

During the snow-free months, elk generally prefer remote areas offering secluded grassy parks surrounded by thick forests of mixed conifers (pine, spruce, and fir) and mountain hardwoods (especially aspen and Gambel oak).

Such areas provide both good escape cover and the mix of foods the big grazers prefer. Elk need very little water in spring and early summer, wringing most of their requirement for liquids from the huge quantities and wide variety of lush vegetation they consume. (According to *The Elk of North America: Ecology and Management,* the wapiti's diet across its entire range includes 111 species of trees and shrubs, 77 species of grasses and 142 species of lichens, ferns, and forbs.) In late summer and fall, however, elk need to drink every day. At such times, isolated springs, seeps, streams, tanks, and other reliable sources of surface water become worthwhile places to watch for wapiti.

Elk avoid bright sunlight and heat; I've seen them bedded down on shaded patches of snow on days so cool that I was chilly in a heavy jacket. For this reason, together with the wary animal's natural instincts for self-preservation, don't expect to find elk out in the open during midday. Parks with lots of fresh elk sign (tracks; dark, soft droppings; cud beds, and such) are good places to watch — from a distance, through binoculars — at first and last light. Between late morning and early evening, the animals will usually be bedded down in the darkest, thickest timber or brush they can find. Consequently, stalking slowly and silently through the woods (if you're good at it) is often more productive during midday than is sitting and waiting.

While the West's most numerous species of deer, the muley, commonly shares the elk's mountain habitat, you'll most often find deer atop hills and ridges, while wapiti prefer to hole up on the slopes, as long as those slopes aren't too steep. The relatively level and heavily timbered benches that lie like giant stair steps between steep slopes in many mountainous regions are among the elk's favorite daytime hangouts. In summer, investigate the shady north-facing slopes; in winter, elk prefer south exposures (not for the sun so much as for the lighter snow cover, and consequently, increased exposure of vegetation).

All of the elk's senses are superb, but smell is by far the most important. I have, on occasion, approached elk that must have heard me crunching toward them through dry woods, and yet paid little heed, apparently taking me for one of their own heavy-footed kind; I have, on rare occasion, had elk spot me at close range and, if I remained absolutely motionless, eventually relax and return to feeding; but I have never had an elk hesitate to beat a hasty retreat once it caught a whiff of me.

With this in mind, always approach an elky area from downwind (a caper that will also help mask the sounds of your approach). Here's the rule of thumb for predicting wind direction in the mountains: On normal days (that is, with no storms on the brew), thermal breezes blow downslope during the cool of morning and evening, and upslope during the heat of the day. Thus, all else being equal, it's generally best to attempt approaching elk from below at the edges of day and from above during midday.

Montana wildlife photographer Alan Carey, whose superb work illustrates this book, feels that hiding and waiting is generally a more profitable strategy than stalking. He recommends that you dress in clothing that blends well with the surroundings (or climb a tree or use a camouflaged blind), and set up to wait downwind of a likely sighting area—such as a watering hole in hot weather, or a mud wallow during the rut. In an article he wrote for the July 1987 issue of *American Country* magazine ("The Nature of Wildlife Photography"), Carey offers additional suggestions for getting near elk and other large wild animals.

Wildlife photography is a form of hunting: To get good photos you must become a good predator. When circumstance requires you to make an open approach to a wild animal, don't charge straight toward it or make direct eye contact. Instead, amble casually toward the subject in a zigzag fashion, appearing to look in another direction while using your peripheral vision to keep track of your quarry. (This technique works especially well in national parks and on refuges where animals have become somewhat inured to the presence of humans.)

You'll never see much wildlife if you can't drag yourself out of bed before daylight in order to be where you need to be, when you need to be there. The primary reason for this is that more wild animals are visible when the day is just dawning; they're still on the move—feeding, hunting and drifting from feeding to bedding areas. Late afternoon is also a good bet—but I've found that on warm days, animals rarely start moving until right at sunset, when the air begins to cool.

And don't forgo getting out just because the weather is lousy. When the weather is bleak, wild animals seem to stay active through more of the day.

To these good suggestions, I would add a few more.

Use your legs. There's no point in lurking about an area the elk aren't using. Walk until you find plenty of fresh elk sign and *then* slow down and get sneaky, or look for a likely spot to set up for a morning or evening wait.

Use binoculars. Not only will binoculars help you to identify those tiny dots moving across a park several hundred yards distant, they'll also allow you to "see through" brush and into deep shadows to determine whether that cream-colored lump just a few dozen yards ahead is the rump of an elk lying in its cud bed, or merely a large rock. I've used binoculars to identify elk standing motionless in heavy cover as close to me as 15 yards — animals which I had failed to recognize for what they were with my naked eyes and would have spooked into flight had I not taken a moment to glass the area before moving on.

Because of their light-gathering properties, binoculars can be even more important in the dim light of early morning and late evening, the two times of day that you're most likely to spot elk in the open. For this reason, if you're serious about viewing wildlife, I recommend investing in a quality pair of 7×50 optics, which gather in far more light than the more common 7×35s and perform beautifully at high noon as well.

Use your ears. Elk are gregarious creatures that do a lot of vocal communicating. During late spring and summer, listen for the catlike mewing of the calves and the louder but similar replies of their mothers (the latter sounding not unlike the two-note call of the red-shafted flicker). Cows also occasionally bugle, especially in the spring, though not nearly so loud or long as do bulls during rut, and a cow's bugle is never followed by grunting. The bulls' autumn bugles, of course, are audible for miles. I have even heard elk gnashing their teeth, which elk rancher Lou Wyman says indicates nervousness or displeasure. A sharp bark followed by a loud crashing sound going away means that you've been detected; the bark, generally issued by a sentry cow, is the standard elk alarm cry.

Alone, the sound of elk crashing through the woods isn't always an indication that the animals have found you out and are fleeing; while elk can move in near silence when they wish to, they don't always bother, especially if they're in a hurry. Therefore, if you feel confident that no cattle or other humans are nearby and could be responsible for the racket, it's always worth investigating. But beware of sneaking up on a bear.

Just last evening (it's late July as I write this), while Carolyn was out with our dog on an evening walk and had gone no more than a quarter of a mile from the cabin, she heard "something big" moving toward them through the forest. Following our standard procedure in such situations, she crouched down, whispered Amigo to her side and the two of them froze. A moment later three bulls came lollygagging by (at this time of year, just prior to the rut, they band together in bachelor groups). The lead bull was the largest of the trio, having antlers of five or six points to the side, still in velvet and so thick that Carolyn said she doubted whether both of her hands would completely encircle the base of one. When the bulls spotted my little family crouched in the open no more than 30 yards below them,

they stopped for a momentary stare, then walked on, apparently not the least bit intimidated.

Use your nose. It's common knowledge that most wild animals have olfactory capabilities far superior to those of humans. To wildlife—let's face it—we stink. With elk, however, things are somewhat more equitable, since they stink too. The species exudes odors so strong and distinct that they frequently can be detected, even by the lame human nose, from a good ways off. In the spring, a cow elk's urine often carries an almost pleasant aroma of licorice or anise (dogs love to wallow in it). In the fall, bulls exude a pungent combination of barnyard funk and sex musk.

You can decrease your own odor by bathing with unscented soaps and shampoos before you go out, wearing clean clothes, and eschewing perfumes, colognes, and other such distinctly human concoctions. If you're really serious, you might visit a sporting goods store for a bottle of a brew made for big game hunters that's said to neutralize human body odors. In spite of these precautions, though, if you get upwind of an elk, it will still smell you—just not quite so readily.

During the season for gun hunting, all elk-behavior bets are off. (Bowhunters, since they are far fewer in number, their weapons are silent, and their woodsmanship is generally more practiced, disturb nature far less.) Once the shooting starts, you can forget about seeing elk in the open or counting on them to follow normal routines. Instead, they'll be holed up in the thickest, most remote country available and feeding and moving about only at night (except when they're surprised and run amok in panic).

For safety's sake, anyone who ventures into the elk woods during gun-hunting season should wear the same fluorescent orange clothing required for hunters—or, better yet, stay at home unless you're hunting.

Finally, during your trips afield, please keep in mind the importance of leaving the wilds and its creatures as undisturbed as possible. One of my greatest backcountry pleasures comes when I can maneuver near enough to a group of elk or other large and exceptionally wary animals to observe their every feature and action, and then disappear (or simply sit quietly and allow the elk to disappear) back into the forest without them ever knowing I was there.

The old mountain wisdom that "elk are where you find them" is undeniably true. But by doing a bit of homework before you leave home, a bit of detective work when you reach elk country, and a good bit of sneaky work afield, you can greatly improve your chances of putting yourself among the elk.

During trips afield, always keep in mind the importance of leaving the wilds and its creatures as undisturbed as possible.

Postscript

As of this writing, Colorado Division of Wildlife District Wildlife Manager Cary Carron and USFS Land Manager Ron Klatt are taking a wait-and-see attitude toward the potentially problematic situation at the Raven Ridge elk wintering grounds. No habitat modification projects are planned now, and none will be considered in the future unless and until problems arise between area landowners and the elk, or damage claims become sufficient to justify the cost of an experimental habitat modification project.

At the Rocky Mountain Elk Foundation, there have been a couple of changes. Northern Field Director Alan Christensen, whose information and criticisms were invaluable in the preparation of this manuscript, has left the foundation. After two years, Alan decided it was time to return to his former employer, the U. S. Forest Service. His new position as regional wildlife biologist in Missoula, Montana, will both further Alan's personal goals and place him in an excellent position to continue working closely with the RMEF.

Dr. Gary Wolfe, former southern field director, has been promoted to director of Field Operations. He well deserves it.

Within a week of having been verbally accosted and then outfoxed by the horselaughing bull, I returned to his secluded valley with hopes of getting a good close look at the boisterous but elusive animal.

Elk are magical beings that represent all that is magnificent in nature and wilderness.

On the first occasion, four days after our initial encounter, I secreted myself before daylight in thick cover deep within his valley and bugled and cow-talked for nearly an hour. Receiving no reply, I finally gave up, stood, and walked out onto an open hillside to have a look around. Just then I heard a single snap, as of a dry twig being trodden on, directly behind me. I turned to see the bull no more than 15 feet distant, walking away, his stubby, supposedly inert, tail wagging rhythmically (something I've seen neither before nor since). Out of frustration, I spoke to the departing bull, pleading for him to come back and asking if he was real or a ghost. But he paid no heed, neither stopping nor breaking into a run. He just walked away.

Two days later I returned a third and final time. Again I entered the valley in the predawn dark, hid in good cover, and bugled my heart out. After half an hour I heard a distant reply, which I judged to originate from at least a mile away. Knowing that rutting bulls will frequently answer a challenging bugle but refuse to come in unless the challenger is close enough to threaten their territorial instincts, I decided to try to close the distance between us before bugling again.

I bolted from my hiding place, scurrying up the bottom of an open drainage that led in the direction of the answering bugle, and had gone no more than a few yards when the bull topped the rise at the head of the same drainage, running full-out in my direction. I froze in my tracks, but too late — he had already spotted me. This time he didn't walk away. He ran.

The horselaughing bull had won — three times running.

Fair enough. I shall pester him no more forever. (Unless, of course, he accosts me again.)

And what of the big red bull? The largest and most remote portion of his favored spring- and summertime turf across the valley from my place is public land, a small green square of America's checkerboard commons. The rest, including the parks and aspen groves in which I've been able to observe him for several seasons now, belongs to a friend of mine named Helen. Helen is an octogenarian rancher who was born and has lived her entire long life on that beautiful land over there, land homesteaded by her parents in the late 1800s.

This summer, as occasionally happens, Helen found it necessary to open the back-pasture gates and allow her cattle to range out onto a wild tag-end of her ranch that normally goes ungrazed, except by the big red bull and his comrades.

And so one bright July morning came the lowing beeves; beeves to fatten in those rich meadows where the big red bull had grazed through the spring and early summer and from which, in previous seasons, he'd bugled his unfettered autumnal lust; beeves to foul the sparkling rills from which the big red bull had quenched his thirst.

The very morning the cows plodded in, the big red bull and his crew pulled out. I can guess that he headed for the less crowded pastures back up on the adjoining BLM lands, but all I know for certain is that I haven't seen or heard him since. Now, instead of ivory-tipped antlers flashing white in the sun and the distinctive cream rump patches of wapiti,

I see only whitefaces, black Angus, and beefalo when I gaze across the way through binoculars.

It would be easy, even tempting, to blame ranchers such as Helen for forcing some 90 percent of all the lower 48's elk to bottle up on public land much of the year. But it's not that simple. I can't fault Helen for doing what she must in order to wrest an increasingly modest living from her own property. Not only is it her right as a landowner to ranch the same acres her parents ranched before her, but by so doing she is actually helping the big red bull and his kin.

How? By keeping a large chunk of prime wildlife habitat out of the hands of real-estate developers. A person less in love with the land than Helen would have sold out long ago, coaxed by the financial pressures weighing on smaller ranchers and farmers today to snap up the quick money proffered by land developers eager to chop scenic acreage into overpriced and undersized subdivision lots.

So long as Helen lives, those green parks and white aspen groves over yonder will remain undivided — superficially marred by cattle from time to time, perhaps, but never overgrazed and so remaining capable of rapid self-healing. Next spring, when this summer's beeves have been reduced to burger, and lupines, dandelions, and blue bells again color the parks, the big red bull just might come back. In fact, so long as this little corner of his kingdom survives — undivided, unbulldozed, undeveloped, and largely unpeopled — I'm certain that he will.

Elk are among our best indicators of wildland's health. Like trout, elk prosper only in the most pristine of natural surroundings — environments that are high, cool, clean, and lonesome. And just as the presence of a strong population of native cutthroats indicates a balanced aquatic world, so do thriving herds of wapiti indicate a land environment that's substantially in harmony with nature.

But elk are more than mere indicators of environmental quality. They are magical beings that represent all that is magnificent in nature and wilderness. By their very presence, elk redefine the landscape. The sunny park or aspen-shaded glen where I encounter elk — or even just find signs of their presence (deep split hoof prints in the duff, a cast antler, a bleached thigh bone, the compressed grass of a cud bed, a pile of black-green droppings, an antler-scarred aspen, the pungent licorice aroma of cow urine in spring, the raunchy stench of a bull in rut) — that place is forever transformed in my mind. That place is sanctified.

In this increasingly unsettled and unsettling world, I know of no greater source of peace and balance than to be alone in the wilderness, among the elk.

Appendix
Recommended Reading

Books

Most of the better popular books on elk have been written by and for hunters. I will make no attempt to review or even to catalog those works here, other than to mention one title I know to be outstanding in its field: *Bugling for Elk,* by Dwight Schuh (Stoneydale Press), was written by a bowhunter who knows the elk well and speaks of it as more than a mere moving target.

Among non-hunting-oriented elk books, I recommend:

Elk of North America: Ecology and Management, the Wildlife Management Institute, Washington, D. C., Jack Ward Thomas and Dale E. Toweill, editors (Stackpole Books, 1982). This 698-page, large-format, hardbound book is the bible in its field. Check it out at your local library (it's usually held in the reference section), or order a copy through any good bookseller (or from the Rocky Mountain Elk Foundation).

Lives of Game Animals, Volume III, by Ernest Thompson Seton (Doubleday, Doran & Co., 1927). One-fourth of a fat, four-volume set, this work is long out of print and now a collector's item. It's hard to locate and probably isn't a book the casual reader will want to buy even if a copy can be located. (I felt fortunate to find a complete set in fairly good shape a while back for $90.) However, most good libraries, especially at colleges and universities having biology departments, will hold a set. Volume III contains

Cow and calf. Yellowstone National Park.

a 46-page study of the wapiti as it existed around the turn of the century, including an examination of two subspecies — the Merriam's and the Eastern — then extant but now extinct. Seton's delightful prose and colorful anecdotes alone make this book a worthwhile read for serious students of the elk.

Racks: The Natural History of Antlers and the Animals That Wear Them, by David Petersen (Capra Press, 1991). My goal with *Racks* was to combine years of personal field observation with a survey of the latest scientific research in a book both authoritative and readable, maybe even enjoyable. Since I wrote it, I'll let elk biologist Dr. Gary Wolfe do the bragging chores: "Whether you're a hunter, biologist, wildlife photographer or just a casual observer of nature, *Racks* is must reading if you're interested in the phenomena of antler growth and development."

Periodicals
Bugle: The Quarterly Journal of the Rocky Mountain Elk Foundation is the only periodical publication devoted entirely to the subject of elk. Published in spring, summer, fall, and winter, this magazine is well written and illustrated in full color with the very best in elk photography and art. *Bugle* is available at newsstands and sporting goods stores throughout the western elk states. Or you can order a subscription (four issues) directly from the Rocky Mountain Elk Foundation (P.O. Box 8249, Missoula, MT 59807).

Bibliography

Carey, Alan D. "The Nature of Wildlife Photography." *American Country,* July 1987.
———— Bozeman, Montana. Personal communications with author, 1987.

Carron, Cary, District Wildlife Manager, Colorado Division of Wildlife, Bayfield and Durango, Colorado. Personal and telephone interviews and correspondence with author, 1987.

Christensen, Alan G. "Renewal." *Bugle: The Quarterly Journal of the Rocky Mountain Elk Foundation,* Spring 1985.
———— "Fifty Years of Pittman-Robertson: A Wildlife Legacy." *Bugle: The Quarterly Journal of the Rocky Mountain Elk Foundation,* Fall 1987.
———— Northern Field Director, The Rocky Mountain Elk Foundation, Troy, Montana. Personal and telephone interviews and correspondence with author, 1986–87.

"Division of Wildlife Facts." Colorado Division of Wildlife, 1987.

Ewy, Leonard. "The Miracle of Antler Growth." *Colorado Outdoors,* March/April 1987.

Geist, Valerius. "The Paradox of the Great Irish Stags." *Natural History,* March 1986.

Hall, E. Raymond, ed. *Mammals of North America,* 2nd edition. New York: John Wiley & Sons Inc., 1981.

Hibler, C. P. "Elaeophorosis in Deer and Elk in the Gila

Forest, New Mexico." *Bulletin of the Wildlife Disease Association,* January 1969.

Kallman, Harmon, ed. *Restoring America's Wildlife.* Washington, D. C.: U. S. Department of the Interior, Fish and Wildlife Service, 1987.

Kelly, Joyce. "Robert Bateman Talks with Joyce Kelly." *Defenders.* (Defenders of Wildlife, Washington, D. C.) March/April 1987.

Klatt, Ron, U. S. Forest Service Land Manager, Pine Ranger District, Bayfield, Colorado. Personal conversations and correspondence with author, 1987.

Krakel, Dean II. *Season of the Elk.* Kansas City, Missouri: Lowell Press, 1976.

Levathes, Louise E. "Mysteries of the Bog." *National Geographic,* March 1987.

McCorquodale, Scott. "In Praise of Cows." *Bugle: The Quarterly Journal of the Rocky Mountain Elk Foundation,* Summer 1987.

McSpadden, J. Walker, ed. *Animals of the World.* Garden City, New York: Doubleday, 1947.

Mott, Beverly, Terrestrial Biologist, Colorado Division of Wildlife, Bayfield and Durango, Colorado. Telephone interview with author, August 1987.

Murie, Olais J. *The Elk of North America.* Jackson, Wyoming: Teton Bookshop Publications, 1979.

Nickel, Don. "The Alaskan Elk — Herd in A Bottle." *Bugle: The Quarterly Journal of the Rocky Mountain Elk Foundation,* Spring 1985.

Orr, Robert T. *Mammals of North America.* Garden City, New York: Doubleday, no date.

Petersen, David L. "The Deer of North America." *The Mother Earth News,* November/December 1985.

———— "Wapiti: Monarch of the West." *The Mother Earth News,* September/October 1986.

Rozek, Michael. "Antlers." *National Wildlife.* October 1985.

Rue, Leonard Lee III. *Sportsman's Guide to Game Animals.* New York: Harper & Row, 1968.

———— "Wildlife Profiles — Elk." *American Hunter,* October 1985.

Russell, Osborne. *Journal of A Trapper:1834–1843.* Edited by Aubrey L. Haines. Lincoln, Nebraska: University of Nebraska Press, 1965.

Schlegel, Mike. "Predators and Elk." *Bugle: The Quarterly Journal of the Rocky Mountain Elk Foundation,* Fall 1985.

Seton, Ernest Thompson. *Lives of Game Animals,* Vol. III. Garden City, New York: Doubleday, Doran & Company, 1927.

Thomas, Jack Ward, and Dale E. Toweill eds. *Elk of North America: Ecology and Management.* Washington, D. C.: Stackpole Books, 1982.

U. S. Department of the Interior. "Pittman-Robertson Program — 50 Years of Success in Restoring America's Wildlife." (News release), 1987.

———— "Pittman-Robertson Program Helps Nongame Animals." (News release), 1987.

———— "Pronghorn Antelope." (News release), 1987.

Ward, Johanna, and David Alberswerth. "Our Ailing Public Rangelands: Condition Report — 1985." Washington, D.C.: The National Wildlife Federation and the

Natural Resources Defense Council.

Wolfe, Gary J. "The Relationship Between Age and Antler Development." In *Antler Development in Cervidae.* Edited by Robert D. Brown. Kingsville, Texas: Caesar Kleberg Wildlife Research Institute, Texas A & I University, 1983.

———— "Old Elk, Trophy Elk." *Bugle: The Quarterly Journal of the Rocky Mountain Elk Foundation,* Fall 1984.

———— "Population Dynamics of the Vermejo Park Elk Herd, with Special Reference to Trophy Management." Unpublished doctoral dissertation, Colorado State University, 1985.

———— Southern Field Director, The Rocky Mountain Elk Foundation, Fort Collins, Colorado. Personal and telephone interviews and correspondence with author, 1986–87.

Wolfe, Gary J., and William R. Lance. "Locoweed Poisoning in a Northern New Mexico Elk Herd." *Journal of Range Management,* January 1984.

Wright, Philip, Chairman Emeritus, Records Committee, The Boone and Crockett Club, Missoula, Montana. Telephone interviews with author, March 1986 and September 1987.

About The Author

David Petersen lives with his wife, Carolyn, in the San Juan Mountains northeast of Durango, Colorado. He is a former Marine Corps helicopter pilot, has been writing full-time since 1976, and presently is senior editor (West) for *Mother Earth News* magazine.

Petersen's other books include *Big Sky, Fair Land: The Environmental Essays of A. B. Guthrie, Jr.* (Northland, 1988), *Racks: The Natural History of Antlers and the Animals That Wear Them* (Capra Press, 1991), and *Among the Aspen* (Northland, 1991).

. . . And Photographer

Alan Carey is a well-known and respected wildlife photographer who has photographed everything from grizzlies to wolves to bald eagles. He is the author and photographer of several Northland publications, including *In the Path of the Grizzly,* in its second printing, and *Twilight Hunters: Wolves, Coyotes & Foxes.* His work has also appeared in *National Wildlife, Smithsonian,* and *National Geographic World.* He lives in Montana.